COMPENDIUM

Catechism
of the

Catholic Church

COMPENDIUM

Catechism
of the
Catholic Church

LIBRERIA EDITRICE VATICANA

- Our Sunday Visitor
Huntington, Indiana

First Printing, March 2006
Current Printing, 2023, published by OSV, Our Sunday Visitor, 200 Noll Plaza, Huntington, IN 46750; www.osv.com; 1-800-348-2440

ISBN: 978-1-68192-955-2 (Inventory No. T2875)

Printed in the United States of America

CONTENTS

PART THREE
LIFE IN CHRIST

PART FOUR
CHRISTIAN PRAYER

NOTE ON THIS PRINTING

In August 2018, Pope Francis promulgated revisions to paragraph 2267 of the *Catechism of the Catholic Church* regarding the death penalty.

Please note this printing of the *Compendium* does not include a revised summary of paragraph 2267, as found on p. 137 (no. 469).

The revised paragraph 2267 in the *Catechism of the Catholic Church* is provided here:

2267.   Recourse to the death penalty on the part of legitimate authority, following a fair trial, was long considered an appropriate response to the gravity of certain crimes and an acceptable, albeit extreme, means of safeguarding the common good.

Today, however, there is an increasing awareness that the dignity of the person is not lost even after the commission of very serious crimes. In addition, a new understanding has emerged of the significance of penal sanctions imposed by the state. Lastly, more effective systems of detention have been developed, which ensure the due protection of citizens but, at the same time, do not definitively deprive the guilty of the possibility of redemption.

Consequently, the Church teaches, in the light of the Gospel, that "the death penalty is inadmissible because it is an attack on the inviolability and dignity of the person",[1] and she works with determination for its abolition worldwide.

---

1   FRANCIS, *Address to Participants in the Meeting organized by the Pontifical Council for the Promotion of the New Evangelization*, 11 October 2017: *L'Osservatore Romano*, 13 October 2017, 5.

MOTU PROPRIO
for the approval and publication of
the *Compendium of the
Catechism of the Catholic Church*

*To my Venerable Brothers the Cardinals, Patriarchs, Archbishops, Bishops,
Priests, Deacons and to all the People of God.*

Twenty years ago, work began on the *Catechism of the Catholic
Church* that had been requested by the extraordinary Assembly of
the Synod of Bishops held on the occasion of the twentieth anniversary of the close of the Second Vatican Council.

I am filled with heartfelt thanks to the Lord God for having given
the Church this *Catechism,* promulgated in 1992 by my venerated and
beloved Predecessor, Pope John Paul II.

The great value and beauty of this gift are confirmed above all
by the extensive and positive reception of the Catechism among
Bishops, to whom it was primarily addressed as a sure and authentic
reference text for teaching Catholic doctrine and, in particular, for
formulating local catechisms. But it was also confirmed by its vast
favorable reception in all segments of the People of God, who have
come to know and appreciate it in more than fifty translations which
to date have been published.

It is with great joy that I now approve and promulgate the *Compendium* of that *Catechism.*

The *Compendium* had been fervently desired by the participants
in the International Catechetical Congress of October 2002, which
gave voice to a need widely felt in the Church. My beloved Predecessor, recognizing this desire, decided in February 2003 to begin
preparation of the text by entrusting the work to a Commission of
Cardinals, over which I presided, and which was assisted by various
experts. In the course of the work, a draft of the *Compendium* was
submitted to all the Cardinals and the Presidents of Conferences of
Bishops, the vast majority of whom evaluated the text favorably.

The *Compendium*, which I now present to the Universal Church, is a faithful and sure synthesis of the *Catechism of the Catholic Church*. It contains, in concise form, all the essential and fundamental elements of the Church's faith, thus constituting, as my Predecessor had wished, a kind of *vademecum* which allows believers and non-believers alike to behold the entire panorama of the Catholic faith.

In its structure, contents and language, the *Compendium* faithfully reflects the *Catechism of the Catholic Church* and will thus assist in making the *Catechism* more widely known and more deeply understood.

I entrust this *Compendium* above all to the entire Church and, in particular, to every Christian, in order that it may awaken in the Church of the third millennium renewed zeal for evangelization and education in the faith, which ought to characterize every community in the Church and every Christian believer, regardless of age or nationality.

But this *Compendium*, with its brevity, clarity and comprehensiveness, is directed to every human being, who, in a world of distractions and multifarious messages, desires to know the Way of Life, the Truth, entrusted by God to His Son's Church.

Through the intercession of Mary Most Holy, Mother of Christ and Mother of the Church, may everyone who reads this authoritative text recognize and embrace ever more fully the inexhaustible beauty, uniqueness and significance of the incomparable Gift which God has made to the human race in His only Son, Jesus Christ, the "Way, the Truth, and the Life" (*Jn* 14:6).

Given on 28 June 2005, the vigil of the Solemnity of the Holy Apostles Peter and Paul, in the first year of my Pontificate.

Benedictus PP XVI

The icon of Christ the *Pantocrator* (he who rules all), of rare artistic beauty, calls to mind the words of the psalmist: "Fairer in beauty are you than the sons of men; grace is poured out upon your lips" (Psalm 45:3).

Saint John Chrysostom applied this praise to the Lord Jesus when he wrote: "The Christ was in the prime of life with the strength of the Spirit and there shone forth in him a twofold beauty, that of soul and body" (PG 52, 479).

With its figurative expression, this icon represents the synthesis of the first ecumenical councils by successfully portraying both the splendor of Jesus' humanity and the brilliance of his divinity.

Christ is clothed in a red tunic covered with a dark blue cloak. The two colors call to mind his twofold nature while the gold reflections call attention to the divine person of the Word. A golden stole, the symbol of his eternal priesthood, falls from his right shoulder. The face, majestic and serene, framed by a thick head of hair and surrounded by a cross bearing halo conveying the Greek trilateral "O Ω N" ("He who is"), recalls the revelation of the name of God in Exodus 3:14. Above and at the sides of the icon, there are the two diliterals: "IC–XC" ("Jesus"—"Christ") which represent the title of the image itself.

The right hand, with thumb and ring finger curved to the point of touching each other (to signify the two natures of Christ in the unity of his person), is held in a typical gesture of blessing. The left hand instead holds fast to the book of the Gospel which is adorned with three clasps, pearls, and precious stones. The Gospel, symbol and synthesis of the Word of God, has also a liturgical significance since in the celebration of the Eucharist a passage from it is read and the very words of Jesus are pronounced at the the consecration.

This image, a sublime synthesis of natural and symbolic elements, is an invitation to contemplate and to follow the Lord. Jesus through the Church, his bride and his mystical body, still continues today to bless the human family and to shed light upon it with his Gospel which is the authentic book of truth, happiness, and salvation for man.

In August of 386 while in a garden, Augustine heard a voice saying "Take and read, take and read" (Confessions, 8,12,29). The *Compendium of the Catechism of the Catholic Church*, as a synthesis of the Gospel of Jesus taught by the Church's catechesis is an invitation to open the book of truth and to read it, even to devour it as did the prophet Ezekiel (cf. Ezekiel 3:1-4).

Theophanos of Crete (1546), *The Icon of Christ*, Stavronikita Monastery (Mount Athos). (Used with permission.)

INTRODUCTION

1.　　On 11 October 1992, Pope John Paul II presented the *Catechism of the Catholic Church* to the faithful of the whole world, describing it as a "reference text"[1] for a catechesis renewed at the living sources of the faith. Thirty years after the opening of the Second Vatican Council (1962-1965), the desire for a catechism of all Catholic doctrine on faith and morals, which had been voiced in 1985 by the extraordinary Assembly of the Synod of Bishops, came to fulfilment.

Five years later, on 15 August 1997, the Pope promulgated the *editio typica* of the *Catechismus Catholicae Ecclesiae* and confirmed its fundamental purpose "as a full, complete exposition of Catholic doctrine, enabling everyone to know what the Church professes, celebrates, lives and prays in her daily life."[2]

2.　　In order to realize more fully the *Catechism's* potential and in response to the request that had emerged at the International Catechetical Congress of October 2002, Pope John Paul II, in 2003, established a Commission under the presidency of Cardinal Joseph Ratzinger, Prefect of the Congregation for the Doctrine of the Faith, which was given the task of drafting a *Compendium* of the *Catechism of the Catholic Church*, as a more concise formulation of its contents of faith. After two years of work, a *draft compendium* was prepared and distributed among the Cardinals and the Presidents of Conferences of Bishops for their consultation. The draft, as a whole, was evaluated positively in the great majority of the responses that were received. Therefore, the Commission proceeded to revise the draft and, taking account of the proposals for improvement that had been submitted, prepared the final text.

3.　　There are three principal characteristics of the *Compendium*: the close reliance on the *Catechism of the Catholic Church*; the dialogical format; the use of *artistic images* in the catechesis.

The *Compendium* is not a work that stands alone, nor is it intended in any way to replace the *Catechism of the Catholic Church*: instead, it refers constantly to the *Catechism* by means of reference numbers

---

1　　John Paul II, Apostolic Constitution *Fidei depositum*, 11 October 1992.
2　　John Paul II, Apostolic Letter *Laetamur magnopere*, 15 August 1997.

printed in the margins, as well as by consistent reliance on its structure, development and contents. In fact, the *Compendium* is meant to reawaken interest in and enthusiasm for the *Catechism*, which, in the wisdom of its presentation and the depth of its spirituality, always remains the basic text for catechesis in the Church today.

Like the *Catechism*, the *Compendium* has four parts, corresponding to the fundamental laws of life in Christ.

The first part, entitled "The Profession of Faith," contains a synthesis of the *lex credendi*, the faith professed by the Catholic Church, as expressed in the Apostles' Creed which is further elaborated by the Nicene-Constantinopolitan Creed. In the liturgical profession of the Creed, the Christian assembly keeps the principal truths of the faith alive in memory.

The second part, entitled "The Celebration of the Christian Mystery," presents the essential elements of the *lex celebrandi*. The proclamation of the Gospel finds its authentic response in the sacramental life, through which Christians experience and witness, in every moment of their existence, the saving power of the Paschal Mystery by which Christ has accomplished our redemption.

The third part, entitled "Life in Christ," recalls the *lex vivendi*, through which the baptized manifest their commitment to the faith they have professed and celebrated, through their actions and ethical choices. The Christian faithful are called by the Lord Jesus to act in a way which befits their dignity as children of the Father in the charity of the Holy Spirit.

The fourth part, entitled "Christian Prayer," summarizes the *lex orandi*, the life of prayer. Following the example of Jesus, the perfect model of one who prays, the Christian too is called to the dialogue with God in prayer. A privileged expression of prayer is the *Our Father*, the prayer that Jesus has taught us.

4.   A second characteristic of the *Compendium* is its dialogical format, reflecting the ancient catechetical literary genre of questions and answers. The idea is to reproduce an imaginary dialogue between master and disciple, through a series of incisive questions that invite the reader to go deeper in discovering ever new aspects of his faith. The dialogical format also lends itself to brevity in the text, by reducing it to what is essential. This may help the reader to grasp the contents and possibly to memorize them as well.

5.   A third characteristic is the inclusion of some artistic images which mark the elaboration of the *Compendium*. These are drawn from the rich patrimony of Christian iconography. The centuries-old conciliar tradition teaches us that images are also a preaching of the Gospel. Artists in every age have offered the principal facts of the mystery of salvation to the contemplation and wonder of believers by presenting them in the splendor of color and in the perfection of beauty. It is an indication of how today more than ever, in a culture of images, a sacred image can express much more than what can be said in words, and be an extremely effective and dynamic way of communicating the Gospel message.

6.   Forty years after the close of the Second Vatican Council and in the year of the Eucharist, this *Compendium* represents an additional resource for satisfying the hunger for truth among the Christian faithful of all ages and conditions, as well as the hunger for truth and justice among those who are without faith. The publication of the *Compendium* will take place on the solemnity of the Holy Apostles Peter and Paul, pillars of the Church universal and exemplary evangelizers of the ancient world. These Apostles saw what they preached and witnessed to the truth of Christ even unto martyrdom. Let us imitate them in their missionary zeal and pray to the Lord that the Church may always follow the teaching of the Apostles, from whom she first received the glorious proclamation of the faith.

20 March 2005, Palm Sunday.

✠ Joseph Cardinal Ratzinger
President of the Special Commission

The Adoration of the Magi (cf. Matthew 2:1-12) is a splendid master-piece which portrays the revelation of Jesus to all peoples. The Incarnation is a gift not only to the faith of Mary, Joseph, the women, the shepherds, and the simple folk of Israel but to the faith of these foreigners who came from the East to adore the newborn Messiah and offer him their gifts.

"On entering the house they saw the child with Mary his mother. They prostrated themselves and did him homage. Then they opened their treasures and offered him gifts of gold, frankincense, and myrrh" (Matthew 2:11).

The magi are the first fruits of the nations who are called to the faith and they approached Jesus not with empty hands but with the riches of their lands and cultures.

The Gospel of Jesus is the word of salvation for all humanity. Saint Leo the Great said: "Let all peoples, represented by the three magi, adore the Creator of the universe and may God be known not just in Judea but through all the earth because everywhere in Israel great is his name (cf. Psalm 75:2)" (*Discourse 3 for the Epiphany*).

The first part of the *Compendium* illustrates the encounter between God and man and the response of faith which the Church gives in the name of all people to the gift of the redeeming incarnation of the Son of God and his divine revelation.

Gentile Da Fabiano (1423), *Adoration of the Magi*, Uffizi Gallery, Florence. (Photo credit: Scala/Art Resource, NY.)

PART ONE
THE PROFESSION OF FAITH

SECTION ONE
I BELIEVE—WE BELIEVE

This illumination presents the complete cycle of the six days of creation up to the temptation of our first parents (cf. Genesis 1-3).

"O LORD, how manifold are thy works! In wisdom hast thou made them all; the earth is full of thy creatures. Yonder is the sea, great and wide, which teems with things innumerable, living things both small and great. There go the ships, and Leviathan which thou didst form to sport in it. These all look to thee, to give them their food in due season. When thou givest to them, they gather it up; when thou openest thy hand, they are filled with good things. . . . Bless the LORD, O my soul!" (Psalm 104:24-28, 35).

The Church at the Easter vigil praises the Lord for the even more wonderful work of the redemption of mankind and the cosmos:

"Almighty ever-living God,
who are wonderful in the ordering of all your works,
may those you have redeemed understand
that there exists nothing more marvelous
than the world's creation in the beginning
except that, at the end of the ages,
Christ our Passover has been sacrificed."
(*Roman Missal*, Easter Vigil, Prayers After the Readings)

Bible of Souvigny, *Illumination on the Days of Creation*, Moulins, Municipal Library. (Photo credit: Erich Lessing/Art Resource, NY.)

1. What is the plan of God for man?

God, infinitely perfect and blessed in himself, in a plan of sheer good- 1-25
ness freely created man to make him share in his own blessed life. In
the fullness of time, God the Father sent his Son as the Redeemer and
Savior of mankind, fallen into sin, thus calling all into his Church
and, through the work of the Holy Spirit, making them adopted children and heirs of his eternal happiness.

CHAPTER ONE
Man's Capacity for God

"You are great, O Lord, and greatly to be praised [. . .] You have   30
made us for yourself and our heart is restless until it rests in you."
(Saint Augustine)

2. Why does man have a desire for God?

God himself, in creating man in his own image, has written upon his 27-30
heart the desire to see him. Even if this desire is often ignored, God 44-45
never ceases to draw man to himself because only in God will he find
and live the fullness of truth and happiness for which he never stops
searching. By nature and by vocation, therefore, man is a religious
being, capable of entering into communion with God. This intimate
and vital bond with God confers on man his fundamental dignity.

3. How is it possible to know God with only the light of human reason?

Starting from creation, that is from the world and from the human 31-36
person, through reason alone one can know God with certainty as 46-47
the origin and end of the universe, as the highest good and as infinite
truth and beauty.

4. Is the light of reason alone sufficient to know the mystery of God?

In coming to a knowledge of God by the light of reason alone man 37-38
experiences many difficulties. Indeed, on his own he is unable to

enter into the intimacy of the divine mystery. This is why he stands in need of being enlightened by God's revelation, not only about those things that exceed his understanding, but also about those religious and moral truths which of themselves are not beyond the grasp of human reason, so that even in the present condition of the human race, they can be known by all with ease, with firm certainty and with no admixture of error.

5. How can we speak about God?

39-43
48-49
By taking as our starting point the perfections of man and of the other creatures which are a reflection, albeit a limited one, of the infinite perfection of God, we are able to speak about God with all people. We must, however, continually purify our language insofar as it is image-bound and imperfect, realizing that we can never fully express the infinite mystery of God.

CHAPTER TWO

God Comes to Meet Man

THE REVELATION OF GOD

6. What does God reveal to man?

50-53
68-69
God in his goodness and wisdom reveals himself. With deeds and words, he reveals himself and his plan of loving goodness which he decreed from all eternity in Christ. According to this plan, all people by the grace of the Holy Spirit are to share in the divine life as adopted "sons" in the only begotten Son of God.

7. What are the first stages of God's Revelation?

54-58
70-71
From the very beginning, God manifested himself to our first parents, Adam and Eve, and invited them to intimate communion with himself. After their fall, he did not cease his revelation to them but promised salvation for all their descendants. After the flood, he made a covenant with Noah, a covenant between himself and all living beings.

8. What are the next stages of God's Revelation?

God chose Abram, calling him out of his country, making him "the 59-64
father of a multitude of nations" (Genesis 17:5), and promising to 72
bless in him "all the families of the earth" (Genesis 12:3). The people
descended from Abraham would be the trustee of the divine promise
made to the patriarchs. God formed Israel as his chosen people, free-
ing them from slavery in Egypt, establishing with them the covenant
of Mount Sinai, and, through Moses, giving them his law. The prophets proclaimed a radical redemption of the people and a salvation
which would include all nations in a new and everlasting covenant.
From the people of Israel and from the house of King David, would
be born the Messiah, Jesus.

9. What is the full and definitive stage of God's Revelation?

The full and definitive stage of God's revelation is accomplished 65-66
in his Word made flesh, Jesus Christ, the mediator and fullness of 73
Revelation. He, being the only-begotten Son of God made man, is the
perfect and definitive Word of the Father. In the sending of the Son
and the gift of the Spirit, Revelation is now fully complete, although
the faith of the Church must gradually grasp its full significance over
the course of centuries.

> *"In giving us his Son, his only and definitive Word, God spoke
> everything to us at once in this sole Word, and he has no more to
> say."* (Saint John of the Cross)

10. What is the value of private revelations?

While not belonging to the deposit of faith, private revelations may 67
help a person to live the faith as long as they lead us to Christ. The
Magisterium of the Church, which has the duty of evaluating such
private revelations, cannot accept those which claim to surpass or
correct that definitive Revelation which is Christ.

THE TRANSMISSION OF DIVINE REVELATION

11. Why and in what way is divine revelation transmitted?

74   God "desires all men to be saved and to come to the knowledge of the truth" (1 Timothy 2:4), that is, of Jesus Christ. For this reason, Christ must be proclaimed to all according to his own command, "Go forth and teach all nations" (Matthew 28:19). And this is brought about by Apostolic Tradition.

12. What is Apostolic Tradition?

75-79   Apostolic Tradition is the transmission of the message of Christ,
83   brought about from the very beginnings of Christianity by means
96, 98   of preaching, bearing witness, institutions, worship, and inspired writings. The Apostles transmitted all they received from Christ and learned from the Holy Spirit to their successors, the bishops, and through them to all generations until the end of the world.

13. In what ways does Apostolic Tradition occur?

76   Apostolic Tradition occurs in two ways: through the living transmission of the word of God (also simply called Tradition) and through Sacred Scripture which is the same proclamation of salvation in written form.

14. What is the relationship between Tradition and Sacred Scripture?

80-82   Tradition and Sacred Scripture are bound closely together and com-
97   municate one with the other. Each of them makes present and fruitful in the Church the mystery of Christ. They flow out of the same divine well-spring and together make up one sacred deposit of faith from which the Church derives her certainty about revelation.

15. To whom is the deposit of faith entrusted?

84, 91   The Apostles entrusted the deposit of faith to the whole of the
94, 99   Church. Thanks to its supernatural sense of faith the people of God as a whole, assisted by the Holy Spirit and guided by the Magisterium of the Church, never ceases to welcome, to penetrate more deeply and to live more fully from the gift of divine revelation.

16. To whom is given the task of authentically interpreting the deposit of faith?

The task of giving an authentic interpretation of the deposit of faith 85-90
has been entrusted to the living teaching office of the Church alone, 100
that is, to the successor of Peter, the Bishop of Rome, and to the bishops in communion with him. To this Magisterium, which in the service of the Word of God enjoys the certain charism of truth, belongs
also the task of defining dogmas which are formulations of the truths
contained in divine Revelation. This authority of the Magisterium
also extends to those truths necessarily connected with Revelation.

17. What is the relationship between Scripture, Tradition and the Magisterium?

Scripture, Tradition, and the Magisterium are so closely united with 95
each other that one of them cannot stand without the others. Working
together, each in its own way, under the action of the one Holy Spirit,
they all contribute effectively to the salvation of souls.

SACRED SCRIPTURE

18. Why does Sacred Scripture teach the truth?

Because God himself is the author of Sacred Scripture. For this rea- 105-108
son it is said to be inspired and to teach without error those truths 135-136
which are necessary for our salvation. The Holy Spirit inspired the
human authors who wrote what he wanted to teach us. The Christian
faith, however, is not a "religion of the Book," but of the Word of
God—"not a written and mute word, but incarnate and living" (Saint
Bernard of Clairvaux).

19. How is Sacred Scripture to be read?

Sacred Scripture must be read and interpreted with the help of the 109-119
Holy Spirit and under the guidance of the Magisterium of the Church 137
according to three criteria: (1) it must be read with attention to the
content and unity of the whole of Scripture; (2) it must be read within
the living Tradition of the Church; (3) it must be read with attention
to the analogy of faith, that is, the inner harmony which exists among
the truths of the faith themselves.

20. What is the *Canon* of Scripture?

120
138   The *Canon* of Scripture is the complete list of the sacred writings which the Church has come to recognize through Apostolic Tradition. The *Canon* consists of 46 books of the Old Testament and 27 of the New.

21. What is the importance of the Old Testament for Christians?

121-123   Christians venerate the Old Testament as the true word of God. All of the books of the Old Testament are divinely inspired and retain a permanent value. They bear witness to the divine pedagogy of God's saving love. They are written, above all, to prepare for the coming of Christ, the Savior of the universe.

22. What importance does the New Testament have for Christians?

124-127
139   The New Testament, whose central object is Jesus Christ, conveys to us the ultimate truth of divine Revelation. Within the New Testament the four Gospels of Matthew, Mark, Luke and John are the heart of all the Scriptures because they are the principal witness to the life and teaching of Jesus. As such, they hold a unique place in the Church.

23. What is the unity that exists between the Old and the New Testaments?

128-130
140   Scripture is one insofar as the Word of God is one. God's plan of salvation is one, and the divine inspiration of both Testaments is one. The Old Testament prepares for the New and the New Testament fulfills the Old; the two shed light on each other.

24. What role does Sacred Scripture play in the life of the Church?

131-133
141-142   Sacred Scripture gives support and vigor to the life of the Church. For the children of the Church, it is a confirmation of the faith, food for the soul and the fount of the spiritual life. Sacred Scripture is the soul of theology and of pastoral preaching. The Psalmist says that it is "a lamp to my feet and a light to my path" (Psalm 119:105). The Church, therefore, exhorts all to read Sacred Scripture frequently because "ignorance of the Scriptures is ignorance of Christ" (Saint Jerome).

CHAPTER THREE
Man's Response to God

I BELIEVE

25. How does man respond to God who reveals himself?

Sustained by divine grace, we respond to God with the obedience   142-143
of faith, which means the full surrender of ourselves to God and the
acceptance of his truth insofar as it is guaranteed by the One who is
Truth itself.

26. Who are the principal witnesses of the obedience of faith in the Sacred Scriptures?

There are many such witnesses, two in particular: One is *Abraham*   144-149
who when put to the test "believed God" (Romans 4:3) and always
obeyed his call. For this reason he is called "the father of all who
believe" (Romans 4:11). The other is the *Virgin Mary* who, throughout
her entire life, embodied in a perfect way the obedience of faith: *"Let
it be done to me according to your word"* (Luke 1:38).

27. What does it mean in practice for a person to believe in God?

It means to adhere to God himself, entrusting oneself to him and giv-   150-152
ing assent to all the truths which God has revealed because God is   176-178
Truth. It means to believe in one God in three Persons, Father, Son,
and Holy Spirit.

28. What are the characteristics of faith?

Faith is the supernatural virtue which is *necessary* for salvation. It is   153-165
a *free gift* of God and is accessible to all who humbly seek it. The act   179-180
of faith is *a human act*, that is, an act of the intellect of a person—   183-184
prompted by the will moved by God—who freely assents to divine
truth. Faith is also *certain* because it is founded on the Word of God;
it *works* "through charity" (Galatians 5:6); and it *continually grows*
through listening to the Word of God and through prayer. It is, even
now, a *foretaste* of the joys of heaven.

29. Why is there no contradiction between faith and science?

159 Though faith is above reason, there can never be a contradiction between faith and science because both originate in God. It is God himself who gives to us the light both of reason and of faith.

> *"I believe, in order to understand; and I understand, the better to believe."* (Saint Augustine)

WE BELIEVE

30. Why is faith a personal act, and at the same time ecclesial?

166-169 Faith is a personal act insofar as it is the free response of the human
181 person to God who reveals himself. But at the same time it is an ecclesial act which expresses itself in the proclamation, we believe. It is in fact the Church that believes: and thus by the grace of the Holy Spirit precedes, engenders and nourishes the faith of each Christian For this reason the Church is Mother and Teacher.

> *"No one can have God as Father who does not have the Church as Mother."* (Saint Cyprian)

31. Why are the formulas of faith important?

170-171 The formulas of faith are important because they permit one to express, assimilate, celebrate, and share together with others the truths of the faith through a common language.

32. In what way is the faith of the Church one faith alone?

172-175 The Church, although made up of persons who have diverse lan-
182 guages, cultures, and rites, nonetheless professes with a united voice the one faith that was received from the one Lord and that was passed on by the one Apostolic Tradition. She confesses one God alone, Father, Son, and Holy Spirit, and points to one way of salvation. Therefore we believe with one heart and one soul all that is contained in the Word of God, handed down or written, and which is proposed by the Church as divinely revealed.

SECTION TWO
THE PROFESSION OF
THE CHRISTIAN FAITH

This ancient mosaic found in the Roman basilica of Saint Clement celebrates the triumph of the cross, the central mystery of the Christian faith. One can observe the luxuriant embellishment of a tuft of acanthus leaves from which come forth so many circlets going out in all directions with their flowers and fruits. This plant takes its vitality from the cross of Jesus whose sacrifice is the re-creation of mankind and the cosmos. Jesus is the new Adam who by the mystery of his Passion, death, and Resurrection brings about the rebirth of mankind and its reconciliation with the Father.

Around the suffering Christ are twelve white doves who represent the twelve Apostles. At the foot of the cross are Mary and John, the beloved disciple:

"When Jesus saw his mother, and the disciple whom he loved standing near, he said to his mother, 'Woman, behold, your son!' Then he said to the disciple, 'Behold, your mother!' And from that hour the disciple took her to his own home" (John 19:26-27).

Above the cross the Father's hand is extended, offering a crown of glory to his Son who by his Paschal Mystery is the victor over death.

At the base of the plant there is a little stag who does battle with the evil serpent.

From this plant which stands for the tree of redemption, there comes forth a spring of gushing water giving life to the four rivulets, symbols of the four gospels, at which the faithful quench their thirst like deer at the springs of living water. The Church is here pictured as a heavenly garden given life by Christ, the true tree of life.

Basilica of Saint Clement, Mosaic in the Apse, Rome. (Photo credit: Scala/ Art Resource, NY.)

THE CREED

The Apostles' Creed

I believe in God,
the Father almighty,
Creator of heaven and earth,
and in Jesus Christ, his only Son, our
    Lord,
who was conceived by the Holy Spirit,
born of the Virgin Mary,
suffered under Pontius Pilate,
was crucified, died and was buried;
he descended into hell;
on the third day he rose again from
    the dead;
he ascended into heaven,
and is seated at the right hand of God
    the Father almighty;
from there he will come to judge the
    living and the dead.

I believe in the Holy Spirit,
the holy catholic Church,
the communion of saints,
the forgiveness of sins,
the resurrection of the body,
and life everlasting. Amen.

Symbolum Apostolicum

Credo in Deum, Patrem
    omnipoténtem,
Creatórem caeli et terrae,
et in Iesum Christum, Filium
    Eius únicum,
Dóminum nostrum,
qui conceptus est de Spiritu Sancto,
natus ex María Virgine,
passus sub Póntio Piláto,
crucifixus, mórtuus, et sepúltus,
descendit ad ínferos,
tértia die resurréxit a mórtuis,
ascéndit ad caelos, sedet ad
    déxteram Dei
Patris omnipoténtis, inde ventúrus est
iudicáre vivos et mórtuos.

Et in Spíritum Sanctum,
sanctam Ecclésiam cathólicam,
sanctórum communiónem,
remissiónem peccatórum,
carnis resurrectiónem,
vitam aetérnam.
Amen.

The Nicene-Constantinopolitan Creed

I believe in one God,
the Father almighty,
maker of heaven and earth,
of all things visible and invisible.

I believe in one Lord Jesus Christ,
the Only Begotten Son of God,
born of the Father before all ages.
God from God, Light from Light,
true God from true God,
begotten, not made, consubstantial with
the Father;
through him all things were made.
For us men and for our salvation
he came down from heaven,

and by the Holy Spirit was incarnate of
the Virgin Mary,
and became man.

For our sake he was crucified under
Pontius Pilate,
he suffered death and was buried,
and rose again on the third day
in accordance with the Scriptures.
He ascended into heaven
and is seated at the right hand of the Father.
He will come again in glory
to judge the living and the dead
and his kingdom will have no end.

I believe in the Holy Spirit, the Lord, the
giver of life,
who proceeds from the Father and the Son,
who with the Father and the Son is
adored and glorified,
who has spoken through the prophets.

I believe in one, holy, catholic and
apostolic Church.
I confess one Baptism for the forgiveness
of sins
and I look forward to the resurrection of
the dead
and the life of the world to come. Amen.

Symbolum Nicaenum-Constantinopolitanum

Credo in unum Deum,
Patrem omnipoténtem,
Factórem caeli et terrae,
visibílium ómnium et invisibílium.
Et in unum Dóminum Iesum
Christum,
Filium Dei unigénitum
et ex Patre natum ante ómnia saécula:
Deum de Deo,
Lumen de Lúmine,
Deum verum de Deo vero,
génitum, non factum,
consubstantiálem Patri:
per quem ómnia facta sunt;
qui propter nos hómines et
proper nostram
salútem, descéndit de caelis,
et incarnátus est de Spíritu Sancto ex
María Virgine et homo factus est,
crucifixus etiam pro nobis
sub Póntio Piláto,
passus et sepúltus est,
et resurréxit tértia die secúndum
Scriptúras,
et ascéndit in cælum, sedet ad
déxteram Patris, et íterum
ventúrus est
cum glória, iudicáre vivos et mórtuos,
cuius regni non erit finis.
Credo in Spíritum Sanctum,
Dóminum et vivificántem,
qui ex Patre Filióque procédit,
qui cum Patre et Fílio simul adorátur
et conglorificátur, qui locútus
est per Prophétas.

Et unam sanctam cathólicam et apos-
tólicam Ecclésiam.
Confíteor unum Baptísma in remissiónem peccatórum.
Et exspécto resurrectiónem
mortuórum,
et vitam ventúri saéculi.
Amen.

CHAPTER ONE
I Believe in God the Father

THE SYMBOLS OF FAITH

33. What are the symbols of faith?

The symbols of faith are composite formulas, also called "professions   185-188
of faith" or "Creeds," with which the Church from her very begin-   192, 197
ning has set forth synthetically and handed on her own faith in a language that is normative and common to all the faithful.

34. What are the most ancient symbols (professions) of faith?

The most ancient symbols of faith are the *baptismal* creeds. Because   189-191
Baptism is conferred "in the name of the Father and of the Son and
of the Holy Spirit" (Matthew 28:19), the truths of faith professed at
Baptism are articulated in reference to the three Persons of the Most
Holy Trinity.

35. What are the most important symbols of the faith?

They are the *Apostles' Creed* which is the ancient baptismal symbol of   193-195
the Church of Rome and the *Nicene-Constantinopolitan Creed* which
stems from the first two ecumenical Councils, that of Nicea (A.D. 325)
and that of Constantinople (A.D. 381) and which even to this day are
common to all the great Churches of the East and the West.

I BELIEVE IN GOD, THE FATHER ALMIGHTY, CREATOR OF
HEAVEN AND EARTH

36. Why does the Profession of Faith begin with the words, "I believe in God"?

The Profession of Faith begins with these words because the affir-   198-199
mation "I believe in God" is the most important, the source of all the
other truths about man and about the world, and about the entire life
of everyone who believes in God.

37. Why does one profess belief that there is only one God?

200-202 228 Belief in the one God is professed because he has revealed himself to the people of Israel as the only One when he said, "Hear, O Israel: The LORD our God is one LORD" (Deuteronomy 6:4) and "there is no other" (Isaiah 45:22). Jesus himself confirmed that God is "the one Lord" (Mark 12:29). To confess that Jesus and the Holy Spirit are also God and Lord does not introduce any division into the one God.

38. With what name does God reveal Himself?

203-205 230-231 God revealed himself to Moses as the living God, "the God of Abraham, the God of Isaac, the God of Jacob" (Exodus 3:6). God also revealed to Moses his mysterious name "I Am Who I Am (YHWH)." Already in Old Testament times this ineffable name of God was replaced by the divine title *Lord*. Thus in the New Testament, Jesus who was called *Lord* is seen as true God.

39. Is God the only One who "is"?

212-213 Since creatures have received everything they are and have from God, only God in himself *is* the fullness of being and of every perfection. God is "He who is" without origin and without end. Jesus also reveals that he bears the divine name "I AM" (John 8:28).

40. Why is the revelation of God's name important?

206-213 In revealing his name, God makes known the riches contained in the ineffable mystery of his being. He alone is from everlasting to everlasting. He is the One who transcends the world and history. It is he who made heaven and earth. He is the faithful God, always close to his people, in order to save them. He is the highest holiness, "rich in mercy" (Ephesians 2:4), always ready to forgive. He is the One who is spiritual, transcendent, omnipotent, eternal, personal, and perfect. He is truth and love.

> "God is the infinitely perfect being who is the most Holy Trinity."
> (Saint Turibius of Mongrovejo)

41. In what way is God the truth?

God is Truth itself and as such he can neither deceive nor be deceived. 214-217
He is "light, and in him there is no darkness" (1 John 1:5). The eternal 231
Son of God, the incarnation of wisdom, was sent into the world "to
bear witness to the truth" (John 18:37).

42. In what way does God reveal that he is love?

God revealed himself to Israel as the One who has a stronger love 218-221
than that of parents for their children or of husbands and wives for
their spouses. God in himself "is love" (1 John 4:8, 16), who gives himself completely and gratuitously, who "so loved the world that he gave
his only Son [so] that the world might be saved through him" (John
3:16-17). By sending his Son and the Holy Spirit, God reveals that he
himself is an eternal exchange of love.

43. What does it mean to believe in only one God?

To believe in the one and only God involves coming to know his 222-227
greatness and majesty. It involves living in thanksgiving and trust- 229
ing always in him, even in adversity. It involves knowing the unity
and true dignity of all human beings, created in his image. It involves
making good use of the things which he has created.

44. What is the central mystery of Christian faith and life?

The central mystery of Christian faith and life is the mystery of the 232-237
Most Blessed Trinity. Christians are baptized in the name of the
Father and of the Son and of the Holy Spirit.

45. Can the mystery of the Most Holy Trinity be known by the light of human reason alone?

God has left some traces of his trinitarian being in creation and in the 237
Old Testament but his inmost being as the Holy Trinity is a mystery
which is inaccessible to reason alone or even to Israel's faith before
the Incarnation of the Son of God and the sending of the Holy Spirit.
This mystery was revealed by Jesus Christ and it is the source of all
the other mysteries.

46. What did Jesus Christ reveal to us about the mystery of the Father?

240-242   Jesus Christ revealed to us that God is "Father," not only insofar as he created the universe and mankind, but above all because he eternally generated in his bosom the Son who is his Word, "the radiance of the glory of God and the very stamp of his nature" (Hebrews 1:3).

47. Who is the Holy Spirit revealed to us by Jesus Christ?

243-248   The Holy Spirit is the third Person of the Most Blessed Trinity. He is God, one and equal with the Father and the Son. He "proceeds from the Father" (John 15:26) who is the principle without a principle and the origin of all trinitarian life. He proceeds also from the Son (*Filioque*) by the eternal Gift which the Father makes of him to the Son. Sent by the Father and the Incarnate Son, the Holy Spirit guides the Church "to know all truth" (John 16:13).

48. How does the Church express her trinitarian faith?

249-256   The Church expresses her trinitarian faith by professing a belief in
266   the oneness of God in whom there are three Persons: Father, Son, and Holy Spirit. The three divine Persons are only one God because each of them equally possesses the fullness of the one and indivisible divine nature. They are really distinct from each other by reason of the relations which place them in correspondence to each other. The Father generates the Son; the Son is generated by the Father; the Holy Spirit proceeds from the Father and the Son.

49. How do the three divine Persons work?

257-260   Inseparable in their one substance, the three divine Persons are also
267   inseparable in their activity. The Trinity has one operation, sole and the same. In this one divine action, however, each Person is present according to the mode which is proper to him in the Trinity.

> *"O my God, Trinity whom I adore . . . grant my soul peace; make it your heaven, your beloved dwelling, and the place of your rest. May I never abandon you there, but may I be there, whole and entire, completely vigilant in my faith, entirely adoring, and wholly given over to your creative action."* (Blessed Elizabeth of the Trinity)

50. What does it mean to say that God is almighty?

God reveals himself as "the strong One, the mighty One" (Psalm   268-278
24:8), as the One "to whom nothing is impossible" (Luke 1:37). His
omnipotence is universal, mysterious and shows itself in the creation
of the world out of nothing and humanity out of love; but above all it
shows itself in the Incarnation and the Resurrection of his Son, in the
gift of filial adoption and in the forgiveness of sins. For this reason,
the Church directs her prayers to the "almighty and eternal God"
("*Omnipotens sempiterne Deus . . .*").

51. What is the importance of affirming "In the beginning God created the heavens and the earth" (Genesis 1:1)?

The significance is that creation is the foundation of all God's saving   279-289
plans. It shows forth the almighty and wise love of God, and it is the   315
first step toward the covenant of the one God with his people. It is the
beginning of the history of salvation which culminates in Christ; and
it is the first answer to our fundamental questions regarding our very
origin and destiny.

52. Who created the world?

The Father, the Son, and the Holy Spirit are the one and indivisible   290-292
principle of creation even though the work of creating the world is   316
particularly attributed to God the Father.

53. Why was the world created?

The world was created for the glory of God who wished to show forth   293-294
and communicate his goodness, truth and beauty. The ultimate end   319
of creation is that God, in Christ, might be "all in all" (1 Corinthians
15:28) for his glory and for our happiness.

> "*The glory of God is man fully alive; moreover man's life is the
> vision of God.*" (Saint Irenaeus)

54. How did God create the universe?

God created the universe freely with wisdom and love. The world is   295-301
not the result of any necessity, nor of blind fate, nor of chance. God   317-320

created "out of nothing" (*ex nihilo*) (2 Maccabees 7:28) a world which is ordered and good and which he infinitely transcends. God preserves his creation in being and sustains it, giving it the capacity to act and leading it toward its fulfillment through his Son and the Holy Spirit.

55. What is divine Providence?

302-306
321

Divine Providence consists in the dispositions with which God leads his creatures toward their ultimate end. God is the sovereign Master of his own plan. To carry it out, however, he also makes use of the cooperation of his creatures. For God grants his creatures the dignity of acting on their own and of being causes for each other.

56. How do we collaborate with divine Providence?

307-308
323

While respecting our freedom, God asks us to cooperate with him and gives us the ability to do so through actions, prayers and sufferings, thus awakening in us the desire "to will and to work for his good pleasure" (Philippians 2:13).

57. If God is omnipotent and provident, why then does evil exist?

309-310
324, 400

To this question, as painful and mysterious as it is, only the *whole* of Christian faith can constitute a response. God is not in any way—directly or indirectly—the cause of evil. He illuminates the mystery of evil in his Son Jesus Christ who died and rose in order to vanquish that great moral evil, human sin, which is at the root of all other evils.

58. Why does God permit evil?

311-314
324

Faith gives us the certainty that God would not permit evil if he did not cause a good to come from that very evil. This was realized in a wondrous way by God in the death and resurrection of Christ. In fact, from the greatest of all moral evils (the murder of his Son) he has brought forth the greatest of all goods (the glorification of Christ and our redemption).

Heaven and Earth

59. What did God create?

Sacred Scripture says, "In the beginning God created the heavens   325-327
and the earth" (Genesis 1:1). The Church in her profession of faith
proclaims that God is the Creator of everything, visible and invisible,
of all spiritual and corporeal beings, that is, of angels and of the visible world and, in a special way, of man.

60. Who are the angels?

The angels are purely spiritual creatures, incorporeal, invisible,   328-333
immortal, and personal beings endowed with intelligence and will.   350-351
They ceaselessly contemplate God face-to-face and they glorify him.
They serve him and are his messengers in the accomplishment of his
saving mission to all.

61. In what way are angels present in the life of the Church?

The Church joins with the angels in adoring God, invokes their assis-   334-336
tance and commemorates some in her liturgy.   352

> *"Beside each believer stands an angel as a protector and shepherd
> leading him to life."* (Saint Basil the Great)

62. What does Sacred Scripture teach about the creation of the visible world?

Through the account of the "six days" of creation Sacred Scripture   337-344
teaches us the value of the created world and its purpose, namely, to
praise God and to serve humanity. Every single thing owes its very
existence to God from whom it receives its goodness and perfection,
its proper laws and its proper place in the universe.

63. What is the place of the human person in creation?

The human person is the summit of visible creation in as much as he   343-344
or she is created in the image and likeness of God.   353

64. What kind of bond exists between created things?

342
354

There exist an interdependence and a hierarchy among creatures as willed by God. At the same time, there is also a unity and solidarity among creatures since all have the same Creator, are loved by him and are ordered to his glory. Respecting the laws inscribed in creation and the relations which derive from the nature of things is, therefore, a principle of wisdom and a foundation for morality.

65. What is the relationship between the work of creation and the work of redemption?

345-349

The work of creation culminates in the still greater work of redemption, which in fact gives rise to a new creation in which everything will recover its true meaning and fulfillment.

Man

66. In what sense do we understand man and woman as created "in the image of God"?

355-358

The human person is created in the image of God in the sense that he or she is capable of knowing and of loving their Creator in freedom. Human beings are the only creatures on earth that God has willed for their own sake and has called to share, through knowledge and love, in his own divine life. All human beings, in as much as they are created in the image of God, have the dignity of a person. A person is not something but someone, capable of self-knowledge and of freely giving himself and entering into communion with God and with other persons.

67. For what purpose did God create man and woman?

358-359
381

God has created everything for them; but he has created them to know, serve and love God, to offer all of creation in this world in thanksgiving back to him and to be raised up to life with him in heaven. Only in the mystery of the incarnate Word does the mystery of the human person come into true light. Man and woman are predestined to reproduce the image of the Son of God made Man, who is the perfect "image of the invisible God" (Colossians 1:15).

68. Why does the human race form a unity?

All people form the unity of the human race by reason of the common   360-361
origin which they have from God. God has made "from one ancestor
all the nations of men" (Acts 17:26). All have but one Savior and are
called to share in the eternal happiness of God.

69. How do the soul and body form a unity in the human being?

The human person is a being at once corporeal and spiritual. In man   362-365
spirit and matter form one nature. This unity is so profound that,   382
thanks to the spiritual principle which is the soul, the body which is
material, becomes a living human body and participates in the dignity of the image of God.

70. Where does the soul come from?

The spiritual soul does not come from one's parents but is created   362-365
immediately by God and is immortal. It does not perish at the moment   366-368
when it is separated from the body in death and it will be once again   382
reunited with the body at the moment of the final resurrection.

71. What relationship has God established between man and woman?

Man and woman have been created by God in equal dignity insofar   369-373
as they are human persons. At the same time, they have been created   383
in a reciprocal complementarity insofar as they are masculine and
feminine. God has willed them one *for* the other to form a communion of persons. They are also called to transmit human life by form-
ing in matrimony "one flesh" (Genesis 2:24). They are likewise called
to subdue the earth as "stewards" of God.

72. What was the original condition of the human person accord-ing to the plan of God?

In creating man and woman God had given them a special participa-   374-379
tion in his own divine life in holiness and justice. In the plan of God   384
they would not have had to suffer or die. Furthermore, a perfect harmony held sway within the human person, a harmony between creature and Creator, between man and woman, as well as between the
first human couple and all of creation.

The Fall

73. How should we understand the reality of sin?

385-389   Sin is present in human history. This reality of sin can be understood clearly only in the light of divine revelation and above all in the light of Christ the Savior of all. Where sin abounded, he made grace to abound all the more.

74. What was the fall of the angels?

391-395   This expression indicates that Satan and the other demons, about
414   which Sacred Scripture and the Tradition of the Church speak, were angels, created good by God. They were, however, transformed into evil because with a free and irrevocable choice they rejected God and his Kingdom, thus giving rise to the existence of hell. They try to associate human beings with their revolt against God. However, God has wrought in Christ a sure victory over the Evil One.

75. What was the first human sin?

396-403   When tempted by the devil, the first man and woman allowed trust
415-417   in their Creator to die in their hearts. In their disobedience they wished to become "like God" but without God and not in accordance with God (Genesis 3:5). Thus, Adam and Eve immediately lost for themselves and for all their descendants the original grace of holiness and justice.

76. What is original sin?

404   Original sin, in which all human beings are born, is the state of depri-
419   vation of original holiness and justice. It is a sin "contracted" by us not "committed"; it is a state of birth and not a personal act. Because of the original unity of all human beings, it is transmitted to the descendants of Adam "not by imitation, but by propagation." This transmission remains a mystery which we cannot fully understand.

77. What other consequences derive from original sin?

405-409   In consequence of original sin human nature, without being totally
418   corrupted, is wounded in its natural powers. It is subject to ignorance,

to suffering, and to the dominion of death and is inclined toward sin. This inclination is called *concupiscence.*

78. After the first sin, what did God do?

After the first sin the world was inundated with sin but God did not abandon man to the power of death. Rather, he foretold in a mysterious way in the "Protoevangelium" (Genesis 3:15) that evil would be conquered and that man would be lifted up from his fall. This was the first proclamation of the Messiah and Redeemer. Therefore, the fall would be called in the future a *"happy fault"* because it "gained for us so great a Redeemer" (Liturgy of the Easter Vigil). 410-412 420

CHAPTER TWO
I Believe in Jesus Christ, His Only Son, Our Lord

79. What is the Good News for humanity?

It is the proclamation of Jesus Christ, the "Son of the living God" (Matthew 16:16), who died and rose from the dead. In the time of King Herod and the Emperor Caesar Augustus, God fulfilled the promises that he made to Abraham and his descendants. He sent "his Son, born of woman, born under the law, to redeem those who were under the law, so that we might receive adoption as sons" (Galatians 4:4-5). 422-424

80. How is the Good News spread?

From the very beginning the first disciples burned with the desire to proclaim Jesus Christ in order to lead all to faith in him. Even today, from the loving knowledge of Christ there springs up in the believer the desire to evangelize and catechize, that is, to reveal in the Person of Christ the entire design of God and to put humanity in communion with him. 425-429

AND IN JESUS CHRIST, HIS ONLY SON, OUR LORD

81. What is the meaning of the name "Jesus"?

430-435
452

Given by the angel at the time of the Annunciation, the name "Jesus" means "God saves." The name expresses his identity and his mission "because he will save his people from their sins" (Matthew 1:21). Peter proclaimed that "there is no other name under heaven given among men by which we must be saved" (Acts 4:12).

82. Why is Jesus called "Christ"?

436-440
453

"Christ" in Greek, "Messiah" in Hebrew, means the "anointed one." Jesus is the Christ because he is consecrated by God and anointed by the Holy Spirit for his redeeming mission. He is the Messiah awaited by Israel, sent into the world by the Father. Jesus accepted the title of Messiah but he made the meaning of the term clear: "come down from heaven" (John 3:13), crucified and then risen , he is the Suffering Servant who gives "his life as a ransom for many" (Matthew 20:28). From the name Christ comes our name of *Christian*.

83. In what sense is Jesus the Only Begotten Son of God?

441-445
454

Jesus is the Son of God in a unique and perfect way. At the time of his Baptism and his Transfiguration, the voice of the Father designated Jesus as his "beloved Son." In presenting himself as the Son who "knows the Father" (Matthew 11:27), Jesus affirmed his singular and eternal relationship with God his Father. He is "the Only Begotten Son of God" (1 John 4:9), the second Person of the Blessed Trinity. He is the central figure of apostolic preaching. The Apostles saw "his glory as of the Only Begotten of the Father" (John 1:14).

84. What is the meaning of the title "Lord"?

446-451
455

In the Bible this title regularly designates God as Sovereign. Jesus ascribed this title to himself and revealed his divine sovereignty by his power over nature, over demons, over sin, and over death, above all by his own Resurrection. The first Christian creeds proclaimed that the power, the honor, and the glory that are due to God the Father also belong to Jesus: God "has given him the name which is above every other name" (Philippians 2:9). He is the Lord of the world and of history, the only One to whom we must completely submit our personal freedom.

WHO WAS CONCEIVED BY THE HOLY SPIRIT, BORN OF THE VIRGIN MARY

85. Why did the Son of God become man?

For us men and for our salvation, the Son of God became incarnate in the womb of the Virgin Mary by the power of the Holy Spirit. He did so to reconcile us sinners with God, to have us learn of God's infinite love, to be our model of holiness and to make us "partakers of the divine nature" (2 Peter 1:4).

456-460

86. What does the word "Incarnation" mean?

The Church calls the mystery of the wonderful union of the divine and human natures in the one divine Person of the Word the "Incarnation." To bring about our salvation the Son of God was made "flesh" (John 1:14) and became truly man. Faith in the Incarnation is a distinctive sign of the Christian faith.

461-463
483

87. In what way is Jesus Christ true God and true man?

Jesus is inseparably true God and true man in the unity of his divine Person. As the Son of God, who is "begotten, not made, consubstantial with the Father," he was made true man, our brother, without ceasing to be God, our Lord.

464-467
469

88. What does the Council of Chalcedon (in the year 451) teach in this regard?

The Council of Chalcedon teaches us to confess "one and the same Son, our Lord Jesus Christ, perfect in his humanity, true God and true man, composed of rational soul and body, consubstantial with the Father by his divinity, and consubstantial with us by his humanity, 'like us in all things but sin' (Hebrews 4:15), begotten from the Father before all ages as to his divinity, and in these last days, for us and for our salvation, born of Mary, the Virgin and Mother of God, as to his humanity."

467

89. How does the Church set forth the Mystery of the Incarnation?

464-469   The Church confesses that Jesus Christ is true God and true man,
479-481   with two natures, a divine nature and a human nature, not confused
with each other but united in the Person of the Word. Therefore, in
the humanity of Jesus all things—his miracles, his suffering, and his
death—must be attributed to his divine Person which acts by means
of his assumed human nature.

> "O Only-begotten Son and Word of God you who are immortal,
> you who deigned for our salvation to become incarnate of the holy
> Mother of God and ever Virgin Mary (. . .) You who are one of
> the Holy Trinity, glorified with the Father and the Holy Spirit,
> save us!" (Byzantine Liturgy of Saint John Chrysostom)

90. Did the incarnate Son of God have a soul with human knowledge?

470-474   The Son of God assumed a body animated by a rational human soul.
482   With his human intellect Jesus learned many things by way of experience; but also as man the Son of God had an intimate and immediate knowledge of God his Father. He likewise understood people's
secret thoughts and he knew fully the eternal plans which he had
come to reveal.

91. How did the two wills of the incarnate Word cooperate?

475   Jesus had a divine will and a human will. In his earthly life the Son of
482   God humanly willed all that he had divinely decided with the Father
and the Holy Spirit for our salvation. The human will of Christ fol-
lowed without opposition or reluctance the divine will or, in other
words, it was subject to it.

92. Did Christ have a true human body?

476-477   Christ assumed a true human body by means of which the invisible
God became visible. This is the reason why Christ can be represented
and venerated in sacred images.

93. What does the heart of Jesus exemplify?

Jesus knew us and loved us with a human heart. His Heart, pierced   478
for our salvation, is the symbol of that infinite love with which he
loves the Father and each one of us.

94. What is the meaning of the expression "conceived by the Holy Spirit . . ."?

This expression means that the Virgin Mary conceived the eternal   484-486
Son in her womb by the power of the Holy Spirit without the coopera-
tion of a man. The angel told her at the Annunciation that "the Holy
Spirit will come upon you" (Luke 1:35).

95. " . . . Born of the Virgin Mary": Why is Mary truly the Mother of God?

Mary is truly the *Mother of God* because she is the Mother of Jesus   495
(John 2:1, John 19:25). The One who was conceived by the power of   509
the Holy Spirit and became truly her Son is actually the eternal Son
of God the Father. He is God himself.

96. What does the "Immaculate Conception" mean?

God freely chose Mary from all eternity to be the Mother of his Son.   487-492
In order to carry out her mission she herself was *conceived immaculate*.   508
This means that, thanks to the grace of God and in anticipation of the
merits of Jesus Christ, Mary was preserved from original sin from the
first instant of her conception.

97. How does Mary cooperate in the divine plan of salvation?

By the grace of God Mary was kept free from every personal sin her   493-494
whole life long. She is the one who is "full of grace" (Luke 1:28), "the   508-511
all holy." When the angel announced to her that she would give birth
to "the Son of the Most High" (Luke 1:32), she freely gave her consent
with "the obedience of faith" (Romans 1:5). Mary thus gave herself
entirely to the person and work of her Son Jesus, espousing whole-
heartedly the divine will regarding salvation.

98. What does the virginal conception of Jesus mean?

496-498 The virginal conception of Jesus means that Jesus was conceived in
503 the womb of the Virgin solely by the power of the Holy Spirit without the intervention of a man. He is the Son of the heavenly Father
according to his divine nature and the Son of Mary according to his
human nature. He is, however, truly the Son of God in both natures
since there is in him only one Person, who is divine.

99. In what sense is Mary "ever Virgin"?

499-507 Mary is ever virgin in the sense that she "remained a virgin in con-
510-511 ceiving her Son, a virgin in giving birth to him, a virgin in carrying
him, a virgin in nursing him at her breast, always a virgin" (Saint
Augustine). Therefore, when the Gospels speak of the "brothers and
sisters of Jesus," they are talking about the close relations of Jesus,
according to the way of speaking used in Sacred Scripture.

100. In what way is the spiritual motherhood of Mary universal?

501-507 Mary had only one Son, Jesus, but in him her spiritual motherhood
511 extends to all whom he came to save. Obediently standing at the side
of the new Adam, Jesus Christ, the Virgin is the *new Eve*, the true
mother of all the living, who with a mother's love cooperates in their
birth and their formation in the order of grace. Virgin and Mother,
Mary is the figure of the Church, its most perfect realization.

101. In what sense is the life of Christ a Mystery?

512-521 The entire life of Christ is a revelation. What was visible in the earthly
561-562 life of Jesus leads us to the *invisible mystery of his divine sonship*: "whoever has seen me has seen the Father" (John 14:9). Furthermore, even
though salvation comes completely from the cross and the resurrection, the entire life of Christ is a *mystery of redemption* because everything that Jesus did, said, and suffered had for its aim the salvation of
fallen human beings and the restoration of their vocation as children
of God.

102. How did God prepare the world for the mystery of Christ?

522-524 God prepared for the coming of his Son over the centuries. He awak-
ened in the hearts of the pagans a dim expectation of this coming and

he prepared for it specifically through the Old Testament, culminating with *John the Baptist* who was the last and greatest of the prophets. We relive this long period of expectancy in the annual liturgical celebration of the season of Advent.

103. What does the Gospel teach about the mysteries of the birth and infancy of Jesus?

At *Christmas* the glory of heaven is shown forth in the weakness of a baby; the *circumcision* of Jesus is a sign of his belonging to the Hebrew people and is a prefiguration of our Baptism; the *Epiphany* is the manifestation of the Messiah King of Israel to all the nations; at the *presentation in the temple,* Simeon and Anna symbolize all the anticipation of Israel awaiting its encounter with its Savior; the *flight into Egypt* and the massacre of the innocents proclaim that the entire life of Christ will be under the sign of persecution; the *departure from Egypt* recalls the exodus and presents Jesus as the new Moses and the true and definitive liberator.

525-530
563-564

104. What does the hidden life of Jesus in Nazareth teach us?

In the course of his *hidden life* in Nazareth Jesus stayed in the silence of an ordinary existence. This allows us to enter into fellowship with him in the holiness to be found in a daily life marked by prayer, simplicity, work and family love. His obedience to Mary and to Joseph, his foster father, is an image of his filial obedience to the Father. Mary and Joseph accepted with faith the mystery of Jesus even though they did not always understand it.

533-534
564

105. Why did Jesus receive from John the "baptism of repentance for the forgiveness of sins" (Luke 3:3)?

To inaugurate his public life and to anticipate the "Baptism" of his death, he who was without sin accepted to be numbered among sinners. He was "the Lamb of God, who takes away the sin of the world" (John 1:29). The Father proclaimed him to be his "beloved Son" (Matthew 3:17) and the Spirit descended upon him. The baptism of Jesus is a prefiguring of our baptism.

535-537
565

106. What do we learn from the temptations of Jesus in the desert?

538-540   The temptations of Jesus in the desert recapitulate the temptation of
566   Adam in Paradise and the temptations of Israel in the desert. Satan
tempts Jesus in regard to his obedience to the mission given him by
the Father. Christ, the new Adam, resists and his victory proclaims
that of his Passion which is the supreme obedience of his filial love.
The Church unites herself to this mystery in a special way in the liturgical season of *Lent*.

107. Who is invited to come into the Kingdom of God proclaimed and brought about by Jesus?

541-546   All are invited by Jesus to enter the Kingdom of God. Even the worst
567   of sinners is called to convert and to accept the boundless mercy of
the Father. Already here on earth, the Kingdom belongs to those who
accept it with a humble heart. To them the mysteries of the Kingdom
are revealed.

108. Why did Jesus manifest the Kingdom by means of signs and miracles?

547-550   Jesus accompanied his words with *signs* and *miracles* to bear witness
567   to the fact that the Kingdom is present in him, the Messiah. Although
he healed some people, he did not come to abolish all evils here below
but rather to free us especially from the slavery of sin. The driving out
of demons proclaimed that his cross would be victorious over "the
ruler of this world" (John 12:31).

109. In the Kingdom, what authority did Jesus bestow upon his Apostles?

551-553   Jesus chose the *twelve*, the future witnesses of his Resurrection, and
567   made them sharers of his mission and of his authority to teach, to
absolve from sins, and to build up and govern the Church. In this college, Peter received "the keys of the kingdom" (Matthew 16:19) and
assumed the first place with the mission to keep the faith in its integrity and to strengthen his brothers.

110. What is the meaning of the Transfiguration?

Above all the Transfiguration shows forth the Trinity: "the Father in   554-556
the voice, the Son in the man Jesus, the Spirit in the shining cloud"   568
(Saint Thomas Aquinas). Speaking with Moses and Elijah about his
"departure" (Luke 9:31), Jesus reveals that his glory comes by way of
the cross and he anticipates his Resurrection and his glorious coming which "will change our lowly body to be like his glorious body"
(Philippians 3:21).

> *"You were transfigured on the mountain and your disciples, as
> much as they were capable of it, beheld your glory, O Christ our
> God, so that when they should see you crucified they would under-
> stand that your passion was voluntary, and proclaim to the world
> that you truly are the splendor of the Father."* (Byzantine Liturgy).

111. How did the messianic entrance into Jerusalem come about?

At the established time Jesus chose to go up to Jerusalem to suffer his   557-560
Passion and death, and to rise from the dead. As the Messiah King   569-570
who shows forth the coming of the Kingdom, he entered into his city
mounted on a donkey. He was acclaimed by the little children whose
shout of joyful praise is taken up in the *Sanctus* of the Eucharistic liturgy: "Blessed is he who comes in the name of the Lord! Hosanna
[save us]!" (Matthew 21:9). The liturgy of the Church opens Holy
Week by celebrating this entry into Jerusalem.

JESUS CHRIST SUFFERED UNDER PONTIUS PILATE, WAS
CRUCIFIED, DIED AND WAS BURIED

112. What is the importance of the Paschal Mystery of Jesus?

The Paschal Mystery of Jesus, which comprises his Passion, death,   571-573
Resurrection, and glorification, stands at the center of the Christian
faith because God's saving plan was accomplished once for all by the
redemptive death of his Son Jesus Christ.

113. What were the accusations by which Jesus was condemned to death?

574-576   Some of the leaders of Israel accused Jesus of acting against the law, the temple in Jerusalem, and in particular against faith in the one God because he proclaimed himself to be the Son of God. For this reason they handed him over to Pilate so that he might condemn him to death.

114. How did Jesus conduct himself in regard to the Law of Israel?

577-582   Jesus did not abolish the Law given by God to Moses on Mount Sinai
592   but he fulfilled it by giving it its definitive interpretation. He himself was the divine Legislator who fully carried out this Law. Furthermore, as the faithful Servant, he offered by means of his expiatory death the only sacrifice capable of making atonement for all the "transgressions committed by men under the first Covenant" (Hebrews 9:15).

115. What was the attitude of Jesus toward the temple in Jerusalem?

583-586   Jesus was accused of hostility to the temple. On the contrary, he ven-
593   erated it as "the house of his Father" (John 2:16); and it was there that he imparted an important part of his teaching. However, he also fore-told its destruction in connection with his own death and he pre-sented himself as the definitive dwelling place of God among men.

116. Did Jesus contradict Israel's faith in the one God and Savior?

587-591   Jesus never contradicted faith in the one God, not even when he per-
594   formed the stupendous divine work which fulfilled the messianic promises and revealed himself as equal to God, namely the pardon-ing of sins. However, the call of Jesus to believe in him and to be converted makes it possible to understand the tragic misunderstand-ing of the Sanhedrin which judged Jesus to be worthy of death as a blasphemer.

117. Who is responsible for the death of Jesus?

595-598   The Passion and death of Jesus cannot be imputed indiscriminately either to all the Jews who were living at that time or to their descen-dants. Every single sinner, that is, every human being is really the cause and the instrument of the sufferings of the Redeemer; and the greater blame in this respect falls on those above all who are Christians and who the more often fall into sin or delight in their vices.

118. Why was the death of Jesus part of God's plan?

To reconcile to himself all who were destined to die because of sin God took the loving initiative of sending his Son that he might give himself up for sinners. Proclaimed in the Old Testament, especially as the sacrifice of the Suffering Servant, the death of Jesus came about "in accordance with the Scriptures." 599-605 619

119. In what way did Christ offer himself to the Father?

The entire life of Christ was a free offering to the Father to carry out his plan of salvation. He gave "his life as a ransom for many" (Mark 10:45) and in this way he reconciled all of humanity with God. His suffering and death showed how his humanity was the free and perfect instrument of that divine love which desires the salvation of all people. 606-609 620

120. How is Jesus' offering expressed at the Last Supper?

At the Last Supper with his Apostles on the eve of his Passion Jesus anticipated, that is, both symbolized his free self-offering and made it really present: "This is my body which *is given* for you" (Luke 22:19; emphasis added), "This is my blood . . . which *is poured out*" (Matthew 26:28; emphasis added). Thus he both instituted the Eucharist as the "memorial" (1 Corinthians 11:25) of his sacrifice and instituted his Apostles as priests of the new covenant. 610-611 621

121. What happened in the Agony in the Garden of Gethsemane?

Despite the horror which death represented for the sacred humanity of Jesus who is "the Author of life" (Acts 3:15), the human will of the Son of God remained faithful to the will of the Father for our salvation. Jesus accepted the duty to carry our sins in his body "becoming obedient unto death" (Philippians 2:8). 612

122. What are the results of the sacrifice of Christ on the cross?

Jesus freely offered his life as an expiatory sacrifice, that is, he made reparation for our sins with the full obedience of his love unto death. 613-617 622-623

This love "to the end" (John 13:1) of the Son of God reconciled all of humanity with the Father. The paschal sacrifice of Christ, therefore, redeems humanity in a way that is unique, perfect, and definitive; and it opens up for them communion with God.

123. Why does Jesus call upon his disciples to take up their cross?

618 By calling his disciples to take up their cross and follow him Jesus desires to associate with his redeeming sacrifice those who are to be its first beneficiaries.

124. In what condition was the body of Christ while it lay in the tomb?

624-630 Christ underwent a real death and a true burial. However, the power of God preserved his body from corruption.

JESUS CHRIST DESCENDED INTO HELL; ON THE THIRD DAY HE ROSE AGAIN FROM THE DEAD

125. What is the "hell" into which Jesus descended?

632-637 This "hell" was different from the *hell* of the damned. It was the state of all those, righteous and evil, who died before Christ. With his soul united to his divine Person Jesus went down to the just in hell who were awaiting their Redeemer so they could enter at last into the vision of God. When he had conquered by his death both death and the devil "who has the power of death" (Hebrews 2:14), he freed the just who looked forward to the Redeemer and opened for them the gates of heaven.

126. What place does the Resurrection of Christ occupy in our faith?

631, 638 The Resurrection of Jesus is the crowning truth of our faith in Christ and represents along with his cross an essential part of the Paschal Mystery.

127. What are the signs that bear witness to the Resurrection of Jesus?

Along with the essential sign of the empty tomb, the Resurrection   639-644
of Jesus is witnessed to by the women who first encountered Christ   656-657
and proclaimed him to the Apostles. Jesus then "appeared to Cephas
[Peter], and then to the twelve. Then he appeared to more than five
hundred brethren at one time" (1 Corinthians 15:5-6) and to others
as well. The Apostles could not have invented the story of the resurrection since it seemed impossible to them. As a matter of fact, Jesus
himself upbraided them for their unbelief.

128. Why is the Resurrection at the same time a transcendent occurrence?

While being a historical event, verifiable and attested by signs and   647
testimonies, the Resurrection, insofar as it is the entrance of Christ's   656-657
humanity into the glory of God, transcends and surpasses history as
a mystery of faith. For this reason the risen Christ did not manifest
himself to the world but to his disciples, making them his witnesses
to the people.

129. What is the condition of the risen body of Jesus?

The Resurrection of Christ was not a return to earthly life. His risen   645-646
body is that which was crucified and bears the marks of his Passion.
However it also participates in the divine life, with the characteristics of a glorified Body. Because of this the risen Jesus was utterly
free to appear to his disciples how and where he wished and under
various aspects.

130. How is the Resurrection the work of the Most Holy Trinity?

The Resurrection of Christ is a transcendent work of God. The three   648-650
Persons act together according to what is proper to them: the Father
manifests his power; the Son "takes again" the life which he freely
offered (John 10:17), reuniting his soul and his body which the Spirit
brings to life and glorifies.

131. What is the saving meaning of the Resurrection?

651-655
658
The Resurrection is the climax of the Incarnation. It confirms the divinity of Christ and all the things which he did and taught. It fulfills all the divine promises made for us. Furthermore the risen Christ, the conqueror of sin and death, is the principle of our justification and our Resurrection. It procures for us now the grace of filial adoption which is a real share in the life of the only begotten Son. At the end of time he will raise up our bodies.

JESUS ASCENDED INTO HEAVEN, AND IS SEATED AT THE RIGHT HAND OF GOD THE FATHER ALMIGHTY

132. What does the Ascension mean?

659-667
After forty days during which Jesus showed himself to the Apostles with ordinary human features which veiled his glory as the Risen One, Christ ascended into heaven and was seated at the right hand of the Father. He is the Lord who now in his humanity reigns in the everlasting glory of the Son of God and constantly intercedes for us before the Father. He sends us his Spirit and he gives us the hope of one day reaching the place he has prepared for us.

FROM THERE HE WILL COME TO JUDGE THE LIVING AND THE DEAD

133. How does the Lord Jesus now reign?

668-674
680
As the Lord of the cosmos and of history, the Head of his Church, the glorified Christ mysteriously remains on earth where his kingdom is already present in seed and in its beginning in the Church. One day he will return in glory but we do not know the time. Because of this we live in watchful anticipation, praying "Come, Lord" (Revelation 22:20).

134. How will the coming of the Lord in glory happen?

675-677
680
After the final cosmic upheaval of this passing world the glorious coming of Christ will take place. Then will come the definitive triumph

of God in the parousia and the Last Judgment. Thus the Kingdom of God will be realized.

135. How will Christ judge the living and the dead?

Christ will judge with the power he has gained as the Redeemer of the world who came to bring salvation to all. The secrets of hearts will be brought to light as well as the conduct of each one toward God and toward his neighbor. Everyone, according to how he has lived, will either be filled with life or damned for eternity. In this way, "the fullness of Christ" (Ephesians 4:13) will come about in which "God may be all in all" (1 Corinthians 15:28). 678-679
681-682

CHAPTER THREE
I Believe in the Holy Spirit

I Believe in the Holy Spirit

136. What does the Church mean when she confesses: "I believe in the Holy Spirit"?

To believe in the Holy Spirit is to profess faith in the Third Person of the Most Holy Trinity who proceeds from the Father and the Son and "who with the Father and the Son is adored and glorified." The Spirit is "sent . . . into our hearts" (Galatians 4:6) so that we might receive new life as sons of God. 683-686

137. Why are the missions of the Son and the Holy Spirit inseparable?

In the indivisible Trinity, the Son and the Spirit are distinct but inseparable. From the very beginning until the end of time, when the Father sends his Son he also sends his Spirit who unites us to Christ in faith so that as adopted sons we can call God "Father" (Romans 8:15). The Spirit is invisible but we know him through his actions, when he reveals the Word to us and when he acts in the Church. 687-690
742-743

138. What are the names of the Holy Spirit?

691-693   "The Holy Spirit" is the proper name of the third Person of the Most Holy Trinity. Jesus also called him the Paraclete (Consoler or Advocate) and the Spirit of Truth. The New Testament also refers to him as the Spirit of Christ, of the Lord, of God—the Spirit of Glory and the Spirit of the Promise.

139. What symbols are used to represent the Holy Spirit?

694-701   There are many symbols of the Holy Spirit: *living water* which springs from the wounded Heart of Christ and which quenches the thirst of the baptized; *anointing* with oil, which is the sacramental sign of Confirmation; *fire* which transforms what it touches; the *cloud,* dark or luminous, in which the divine glory is revealed; the *imposition of hands* by which the Holy Spirit is given; the *dove* which descended on Christ at his baptism and remained with him.

140. What does it mean that the Spirit "has spoken through the prophets"?

687-688   The term *"prophets"* means those who were inspired by the Holy Spirit
702-706   to speak in the name of God. The Spirit brings the prophecies of the
743   Old Testament to their complete fulfillment in Christ whose mystery he reveals in the New Testament.

141. What did the Holy Spirit accomplish in John the Baptist?

717-720   The Spirit filled John the Baptist, who was the last prophet of the Old Testament. Under his inspiration John was sent to "prepare for the Lord a people well disposed" (Luke 1:17). He was to proclaim the coming of Christ, the Son of God, upon whom he saw the Spirit descend and remain, the one who "baptizes with the Holy Spirit" (John 1:33).

142. What is the work of the Spirit in Mary?

721-726   The Holy Spirit brought to fulfillment in Mary all the waiting and
744   the preparation of the Old Testament for the coming of Christ. In a singular way he filled her with grace and made her virginity fruitful so that she could give birth to the Son of God made flesh. He made her the Mother of the "whole Christ," that is, of Jesus the Head and of the Church his body. Mary was present with the twelve on the day of

Pentecost when the Holy Spirit inaugurated the "last days" with the manifestation of the Church.

143. What is the relationship between the Spirit and Christ Jesus in his earthly mission?

Beginning with his Incarnation, the Son of God was consecrated in his humanity as the Messiah by means of the anointing of the Spirit. He revealed the Spirit in his teaching, fulfilled the promises made to the Fathers, and bestowed him upon the Church at its birth when he breathed on the Apostles after the Resurrection. 727-730
745-746

144. What happened at Pentecost?

Fifty days after the Resurrection at Pentecost the glorified Jesus Christ poured out the Spirit in abundance and revealed him as a divine Person so that the Holy Trinity was fully manifest. The mission of Christ and of the Spirit became the mission of the Church which is sent to proclaim and spread the mystery of the communion of the Holy Trinity. 731-732
738

> "We have seen the true Light, we have received the heavenly Spirit, we have found the true faith: we adore the indivisible Trinity, who has saved us." (Byzantine Liturgy, Troparion of Vespers of Pentecost)

145. What does the Spirit do in the Church?

The Spirit builds, animates and sanctifies the Church. As the Spirit of Love, he restores to the baptized the divine likeness that was lost through sin and causes them to live in Christ the very life of the Holy Trinity. He sends them forth to bear witness to the Truth of Christ and he organizes them in their respective functions so that all might bear "the fruit of the Spirit" (Galatians 5:22). 733-741
747

146. How do Christ and his Spirit act in the hearts of the faithful?

Christ communicates his Spirit and the grace of God through the *sacraments* to all the members of the Church, who thus bear the fruits of the *new life* of the Spirit. The Holy Spirit is also the Master of *prayer*. 738-741

I Believe in the Holy Catholic Church

The Church in the Plan of God

147. What does the word *Church* mean?

751-752
777, 804
The word *Church* refers to the people whom God calls and gathers together from every part of the earth. They form the assembly of those who through faith and Baptism have become children of God, members of Christ, and temples of the Holy Spirit.

148. Are there other names and images with which the Bible speaks about the Church?

753-757
In Sacred Scripture we find many images which bring out various complementary aspects of the mystery of the Church. The Old Testament favors those images that are bound to the *people of God*. The New Testament offers images that are linked to Christ as the Head of this people which is his Body. Other images are drawn from pastoral life (sheepfold, flock, sheep), from agriculture (field, olive grove, vineyard), from construction (dwelling place, stone, temple), and from family life (spouse, mother, family).

149. What is the origin and the fulfillment of the Church?

758-766
778
The Church finds her origin and fulfillment in the eternal plan of God. She was prepared for in the Old Covenant with the election of Israel, the sign of the future gathering of all the nations. Founded by the words and actions of Jesus Christ, fulfilled by his redeeming death and Resurrection, the Church has been manifested as the mystery of salvation by the outpouring of the Holy Spirit at Pentecost. She will be perfected in the glory of heaven as the assembly of all the redeemed of the earth.

150. What is the mission of the Church?

767-769
The mission of the Church is to proclaim and establish the Kingdom of God begun by Jesus Christ among all peoples. The Church constitutes on earth the seed and beginning of this salvific Kingdom.

151. In what way is the Church a *mystery*?

The Church is a mystery in as much as in her visible reality there is 770-773
present and active a divine spiritual reality which can only be seen 779
with the eyes of faith.

152. What does it mean to say that the Church is the universal sacrament of salvation?

This means that she is the sign and instrument both of the reconcilia- 774-776
tion and communion of all of humanity with God and of the unity of 780
the entire human race.

*The Church: People of God, Body of Christ,
Temple of the Spirit*

153. Why is the Church the "people of God"?

The Church is the "people of God" because it pleased God to sanctify 781
and save men not in isolation but by making them into one people 802-804
gathered together by the unity of the Father and the Son and the
Holy Spirit.

154. What are the characteristics of the people of God?

One becomes a member of this people through faith in Christ and 782
Baptism. This people has for its *origin* God the Father; for its *head* Jesus
Christ; for its *hallmark* the dignity and freedom of the sons of God; for
its *law* the new commandment of love; for its *mission* to be the salt of
the earth and the light of the world; and for its *destiny* the Kingdom of
God, already begun on earth.

155. In what way does the people of God share in the three functions of Christ as Priest, Prophet and King?

The people of God participate in Christ's *priestly* office insofar as the 783-786
baptized are consecrated by the Holy Spirit to offer spiritual sacrifices. They share in Christ's *prophetic* office when with a supernatural sense of faith they adhere unfailingly to that faith and deepen
their understanding and witness to it. The people of God share in his
kingly office by means of service, imitating Jesus Christ who as King

of the universe made himself the servant of all, especially the poor and the suffering.

156. In what way is the Church the body of Christ?

787-791
805-806

The risen Christ unites his faithful people to himself in an intimate way by means of the Holy Spirit. In this way, those who believe in Christ, in as much as they are close to him especially in the Eucharist, are united among themselves in charity. They form one body, the Church, whose unity is experienced in the diversity of its members and its functions.

157. Who is the Head of this body?

792-795
807

Christ "is the head of the body, the church" (Colossians 1:18). The Church lives from him, in him and for him. Christ and the Church make up the "whole Christ" (Saint Augustine); "Head and members form, as it were, one and the same mystical person" (Saint Thomas Aquinas).

158. Why is the Church called the "Bride of Christ"?

796
808

She is called the "Bride of Christ" because the Lord himself called himself her "Spouse" (Mark 2:19). The Lord has loved the Church and has joined her to himself in an everlasting covenant. He has given himself up for her in order to purify her with his blood and "sanctify her" (Ephesians 5:26), making her the fruitful mother of all the children of God. While the term "body" expresses the unity of the "head" with the members, the term "bride" emphasizes the distinction of the two in their personal relationship.

159. Why is the Church called the temple of the Holy Spirit?

797-798
809-810

She is so called because the Holy Spirit resides in the body which is the Church, in her Head and in her members. He also builds up the Church in charity by the Word of God, the sacraments, the virtues, and *charisms*.

> *"What the soul is to the human body, the Holy Spirit is to the members of Christ, that is, the body of Christ, which is the Church."* (Saint Augustine)

160. What are charisms?

Charisms are special gifts of the Holy Spirit which are bestowed   799-801
on individuals for the good of others, the needs of the world, and
in particular for the building up of the Church. The discernment of
charisms is the responsibility of the Magisterium.

The Church Is One, Holy, Catholic, and Apostolic

161. Why is the Church *one*?

The Church is one because she has as her source and exemplar the   813-815
unity of the Trinity of Persons in one God. As her Founder and Head,   866
Jesus Christ re-established the unity of all people in one body. As her
soul, the Holy Spirit unites all the faithful in communion with Christ.
The Church has but one faith, one sacramental life, one apostolic succession, one common hope, and one and the same charity.

162. Where does the one Church of Christ subsist?

The one Church of Christ, as a society constituted and organized   816
in the world, subsists in (*subsistit in*) the Catholic Church, governed   870
by the Successor of Peter and the bishops in communion with him.
Only through this Church can one obtain the fullness of the means
of salvation since the Lord has entrusted all the blessings of the New
Covenant to the apostolic college alone whose head is Peter.

163. How are non-Catholic Christians to be considered?

In the churches and ecclesial communities which are separated from   817-819
full communion with the Catholic Church, many elements of sanctification and truth can be found. All of these blessings come from
Christ and lead to Catholic unity. Members of these churches and
communities are incorporated into Christ by Baptism and so we recognize them as brothers.

164. How does one commit oneself to work for the unity of Christians?

The desire to restore the unity of all Christians is a gift from Christ   820-822
and a call of the Spirit. This desire involves the entire Church and it is   866

pursued by conversion of heart, prayer, fraternal knowledge of each other and theological dialogue.

165. In what way is the Church *holy*?

823-829
867
The Church is holy insofar as the Most Holy God is her author. Christ has given himself for her to sanctify her and make her a source of sanctification. The Holy Spirit gives her life with charity. In the Church one finds the fullness of the means of salvation. Holiness is the vocation of each of her members and the purpose of all her activities. The Church counts among her members the Virgin Mary and numerous Saints who are her models and intercessors. The holiness of the Church is the fountain of sanctification for her children who here on earth recognize themselves as sinners ever in need of conversion and purification.

166. Why is the Church called *"Catholic"*?

830-831
868
The Church is *catholic*, that is *universal*, insofar as Christ is present in her: "Where there is Christ Jesus, there is the Catholic Church" (Saint Ignatius of Antioch). The Church proclaims the fullness and the totality of the faith; she bears and administers the fullness of the means of salvation; she is sent out by Christ on a mission to the whole of the human race.

167. Is the particular Church catholic?

832-835
Every *particular* Church (that is, a *diocese* or *eparchy*) is catholic. It is formed by a community of Christians who are in communion of faith and of the sacraments both with their bishop, who is ordained in apostolic succession, and with the Church of Rome which "presides in charity" (Saint Ignatius of Antioch).

168. Who belongs to the Catholic Church?

836-838
All human beings in various ways belong to or are ordered to the Catholic unity of the people of God. Fully incorporated into the Catholic Church are those who, possessing the Spirit of Christ, are joined to the Church by the bonds of the profession of faith, the sacraments, ecclesiastical government and communion. The baptized who

do not enjoy full Catholic unity are in a certain, although imperfect, communion with the Catholic Church.

169. What is the relationship of the Catholic Church with the Jewish people?

The Catholic Church recognizes a particular link with the Jewish 839-840 people in the fact that God chose them before all others to receive his Word. To the Jewish people belong "the sonship, the glory, the covenants, the giving of the law, the worship, the promises, and the patriarchs; and of their race, according to the flesh, is the Christ" (Romans 9:4, 5). The Jewish faith, unlike other non-Christian religions, is already a response to the revelation of God in the Old Covenant.

170. What is the bond that exists between the Catholic Church and non-Christian religions?

There is a bond between all peoples which comes especially from 841-845 the common origin and end of the entire human race. The Catholic Church recognizes that whatever is good or true in other religions comes from God and is a reflection of his truth. As such it can prepare for the acceptance of the Gospel and act as a stimulus toward the unity of humanity in the Church of Christ.

171. What is the meaning of the affirmation "Outside the Church there is no salvation"?

This means that all salvation comes from Christ, the Head, through 846-848 the Church which is his body. Hence they cannot be saved who, knowing the Church as founded by Christ and necessary for salvation, would refuse to enter her or remain in her. At the same time, thanks to Christ and to his Church, those who through no fault of their own do not know the Gospel of Christ and his Church but sincerely seek God and, moved by grace, try to do his will as it is known through the dictates of conscience can attain eternal salvation.

172. Why must the Church proclaim the Gospel to the whole world?

The Church must do so because Christ has given the command: "Go 849-851 therefore and make disciples of all nations, baptizing them in the name of the Father and of the Son and of the Holy Spirit" (Matthew 28:19). This missionary mandate of the Lord has its origin in the eternal love of God who has sent his Son and the Holy Spirit because he "desires all men to be saved and to come to the knowledge of the truth" (1 Timothy 2:4).

173. In what sense is the Church missionary?

852-856 The Church, guided by the Holy Spirit, continues the mission of Christ himself in the course of history. Christians must, therefore, proclaim to everyone the Good News borne by Christ; and, following his path, they must be ready for self-sacrifice, even unto martyrdom.

174. Why is the Church *apostolic*?

857
869 The Church is apostolic in her *origin* because she has been built on "the foundation of the apostles" (Ephesians 2:20). She is apostolic in her *teaching* which is the same as that of the Apostles. She is apostolic by reason of her *structure* insofar as she is taught, sanctified, and guided until Christ returns by the Apostles through their successors who are the bishops in communion with the successor of Peter.

175. In what does the mission of the Apostles consist?

858-861 The word *"Apostle"* means "one who is sent." Jesus, the One sent by the Father, called to himself twelve of his disciples and appointed them as his Apostles, making them the chosen witnesses of his Resurrection and the foundation of his Church. He gave them the command to continue his own mission saying, "As the Father has sent me, even so I send you" (John 20:21); and he promised to remain with them until the end of the world.

176. What is apostolic succession?

861-865 Apostolic succession is the transmission by means of the sacrament of Holy Orders of the mission and power of the Apostles to their successors, the bishops. Thanks to this transmission the Church remains in communion of faith and life with her origin, while through the centuries she carries on her apostolate for the spread of the Kingdom of Christ on earth.

The Faithful: Hierarchy, Laity, Consecrated Life

177. Who are the faithful?

The Christian faithful are those who, inasmuch as they have been 871-872
incorporated in Christ through Baptism, have been constituted as 934
the people of God; for this reason, since they have become sharers
in Christ's priestly, prophetic and royal office in their own manner,
they are called to exercise the mission which God has entrusted to
the Church. There exists a true equality among them in their dignity
as children of God.

178. How are the people of God formed?

Among the faithful by divine institution there exist *sacred ministers* 873
who have received the sacrament of Holy Orders and who form the
hierarchy of the Church. The other members of the Church are called
the *laity*. In both the hierarchy and the laity there are certain of the
faithful who are *consecrated* in a special manner to God by the profession of the evangelical counsels: chastity or celibacy, poverty, and
obedience.

179. Why did Christ institute an ecclesiastical hierarchy?

Christ instituted an ecclesiastical hierarchy with the mission of feed- 874-877
ing the people of God in his name and for this purpose gave it author- 935
ity. The hierarchy is formed of sacred ministers: bishops, priests, and
deacons. Thanks to the sacrament of Orders, bishops and priests act
in the exercise of their ministry in the name and person of Christ the
Head. Deacons minister to the people of God in the *diakonia* (service)
of word, liturgy, and charity.

180. How is the collegial dimension of Church ministry carried out?

After the example of the twelve Apostles who were chosen and sent 877
out together by Christ, the unity of the Church's hierarchy is at the
service of the communion of all the faithful. Every bishop exercises
his ministry as a member of the episcopal college in communion with
the Pope and shares with him in the care of the universal Church.

Priests exercise their ministry in the presbyterate of the local Church in communion with their own bishop and under his direction.

181. Why does ecclesial ministry also have a personal character?

878-879 Ecclesial ministry also has a personal character inasmuch as each minister, in virtue of the sacrament of Holy Orders, is responsible before Christ who called him personally and conferred on him his mission.

182. What is the mission of the Pope?

881-882
936-937
The Pope, Bishop of Rome and the Successor of Saint Peter, is the perpetual, visible source and foundation of the unity of the Church. He is the vicar of Christ, the head of the College of Bishops and pastor of the universal Church over which he has by divine institution full, supreme, immediate, and universal power.

183. What is the competence of the College of Bishops?

883-885 The College of Bishops in union with the Pope, and never without him, also exercises supreme and full authority over the Church.

184. How do the bishops carry out their mission of teaching?

888-890
939
Since they are authentic witnesses of the apostolic faith and are invested with the authority of Christ, the bishops in union with the Pope have the duty of proclaiming the Gospel faithfully and authoritatively to all. By means of a supernatural sense of faith, the people of God unfailingly adhere to the faith under the guidance of the living Magisterium of the Church.

185. When is the infallibility of the Magisterium exercised?

891 Infallibility is exercised when the Roman Pontiff, in virtue of his office as the Supreme Pastor of the Church, or the College of Bishops, in union with the Pope especially when joined together in an Ecumenical Council, proclaim by a definitive act a doctrine pertaining to faith or morals. Infallibility is also exercised when the Pope and Bishops in their ordinary Magisterium are in agreement in proposing a doctrine as definitive. Every one of the faithful must adhere to such teaching with the obedience of faith.

186. How do Bishops exercise their ministry of sanctification?

Bishops sanctify the Church by dispensing the grace of Christ by 893
their ministry of the word and the sacraments, especially the Holy
Eucharist, and also by their prayers, their example and their work.

187. How do the Bishops exercise their function of governing?

Every bishop, insofar as he is a member of the College of Bishops, 894-896
bears collegially the care for all particular Churches and for the entire
Church along with all the other bishops who are united to the Pope. A
bishop to whom a particular Church has been entrusted governs that
Church with the authority of his own sacred power which is ordinary and immediate and exercised in the name of Christ, the Good
Shepherd, in communion with the entire Church and under the guidance of the Successor of Peter.

188. What is the vocation of the lay faithful?

The lay faithful have as their own vocation to seek the Kingdom of 897-900
God by illuminating and ordering temporal affairs according to the 940
plan of God. They carry out in this way their call to holiness and to
the apostolate, a call given to all the baptized.

189. How do the lay faithful participate in the priestly office of Christ?

They participate in it especially in the Eucharist by offering as a spiri- 901-903
tual sacrifice "acceptable to God through Jesus Christ" (1 Peter 2:5)
their own lives with all of their works, their prayers, their apostolic
undertakings, their family life, their daily work and hardships borne
with patience and even their consolations of spirit and body. In this
way, even the laity, dedicated to Christ and consecrated by the Holy
Spirit, offer to God the world itself.

190. How does the laity participate in the prophetic office?

They participate in it by welcoming evermore in faith the Word of 904-907
Christ and proclaiming it to the world by the witness of their lives, 942
their words, their evangelizing action, and by catechesis. This evangelizing action acquires a particular efficacy because it is accomplished in the ordinary circumstances of the world.

191. How do they participate in the kingly office?

908-913 The laity participate in the kingly function of Christ because they have
943 received from him the power to overcome sin in themselves and in the
world by self-denial and the holiness of their lives. They exercise various ministries at the service of the community and they imbue temporal activities and the institutions of society with moral values.

192. What is the consecrated life?

914-916 The consecrated life is a state of life recognized by the Church. It is a
944 free response to a special call from Christ by which those consecrated give themselves completely to God and strive for the perfection of charity moved by the Holy Spirit. This consecration is characterized by the practice of the evangelical counsels.

193. What can the consecrated life give to the mission of the Church?

931-933 The consecrated life participates in the mission of the Church by
945 means of a complete dedication to Christ and to one's brothers and sisters witnessing to the hope of the heavenly Kingdom.

I Believe in the Communion of Saints

194. What is the meaning of the "communion of saints"?

946-953 This expression indicates first of all the common sharing of all the
960 members of the Church in holy things (*sancta*): the faith, the sacraments, especially the Eucharist, the charisms, and the other spiritual gifts. At the root of this communion is love which "does not seek its own interests" (1 Corinthians 13:5) but leads the faithful to "hold everything in common" (Acts 4:32), even to put one's own material goods at the service of the most poor.

195. What else does "the communion of saints" mean?

954-959 This expression also refers to the communion between holy per-
961-962 sons (*sancti*); that is, between those who by grace are united to the dead and risen Christ. Some are pilgrims on the earth; others, having passed from this life, are undergoing purification and are helped also

by our prayers. Others already enjoy the glory of God and intercede for us. All of these together form in Christ one family, the Church, to the praise and glory of the Trinity.

Mary, Mother of Christ, Mother of the Church

196. In what sense is the Blessed Virgin Mary the Mother of the Church?

The Blessed Virgin Mary is the Mother of the Church in the order 963-964
of grace because she gave birth to Jesus, the Son of God, the Head 973
of the body which is the Church. When he was dying on the cross
Jesus gave his mother to his disciple with the words, "Behold, your
mother" (John 19:27).

197. How does the Virgin Mary help the Church?

After the Ascension of her Son, the Virgin Mary aided the begin- 967-970
nings of the Church with her prayers. Even after her Assumption into
heaven, she continues to intercede for her children, to be a model of
faith and charity for all, and to exercise over them a salutary influ-
ence deriving from the superabundant merits of Christ. The faithful see in Mary an image and an anticipation of the resurrection that
awaits them and they invoke her as advocate, helper, benefactress and
mediatrix.

198. What kind of devotion is directed to the holy Virgin?

It is a singular kind of devotion which differs essentially from the cult 971
of adoration given only to the Most Holy Trinity. This special veneration directed to Mary finds particular expression in the liturgical
feasts dedicated to the Mother of God and in Marian prayers such as
the holy Rosary which is a compendium of the whole Gospel.

199. In what way is the Blessed Virgin Mary the eschatological icon of the Church?

Looking upon Mary, who is completely holy and already glorified 972
in body and soul, the Church contemplates in her what she herself 974-975

is called to be on earth and what she will be in the homeland of heaven.

200. How are sins remitted?

976-980   The first and chief sacrament for the forgiveness of sins is Baptism.
984-985   For those sins committed after Baptism, Christ instituted the sacrament of Reconciliation or Penance through which a baptized person is reconciled with God and with the Church.

201. Why does the Church have the power to forgive sins?

981-983   The Church has the mission and the power to forgive sins because
986-987   Christ himself has conferred it upon her: "Receive the Holy Spirit. If you forgive the sins of any, they are forgiven; if you retain the sins of any, they are retained" (John 20:22-23).

I BELIEVE IN THE RESURRECTION OF THE BODY

202. What is the meaning of the term "body" (or *"flesh"*) and what importance does it have?

990   The resurrection of the *flesh* is the literal formulation in the Apostles
1015   Creed for the resurrection of the body. The term "flesh" refers to humanity in its state of weakness and mortality. "The flesh is the hinge of salvation" (Tertullian). We believe in God the Creator of the flesh; we believe in the Word made flesh in order to redeem flesh; and we believe in the resurrection of flesh which is the fulfillment of both the creation and the redemption of the flesh.

203. What is meant by the "resurrection of the body"?

990   This means that the definitive state of man will not be one in which his spiritual soul is separated from his body. Even our mortal bodies will one day come to life again.

204. What is the relationship between the Resurrection of Christ and our resurrection?

Just as Christ is truly risen from the dead and now lives forever, so he   988-991
himself will raise everyone on the last day with an incorruptible body: 1002-1003
"Those who have done good, to the resurrection of life, and those who
have done evil, to the resurrection of condemnation" (John 5:29).

205. What happens to our body and our soul after death?

After death, which is the separation of the body and the soul, the body   992-1004
becomes corrupt while the soul, which is immortal, goes to meet the   1016-1018
judgment of God and awaits its reunion with the body when it will
rise transformed at the time of the return of the Lord. *How* the resurrection of the body will come about exceeds the possibilities of our
imagination and understanding.

206. What does it mean to die in Christ Jesus?

Dying in Christ Jesus means to die in the state of God's grace without   1005-1014
any mortal sin. A believer in Christ, following his example, is thus   1019
able to transform his own death into an act of obedience and love for
the Father. "This saying is sure: If we have died with him, we will
also live with him" (2 Timothy 2:11).

I Believe in Life Everlasting

207. What is life everlasting?

Eternal life is that life which begins immediately after death. It will   1020
have no end. It will be preceded for each person by a particular judg-   1051
ment at the hands of Christ who is the Judge of the living and the dead.
This particular judgement will be confirmed in the final judgment.

208. What is the particular judgment?

It is the judgment of immediate retribution which each one after   1021-1022
death will receive from God in his immortal soul in accord with his   1051
faith and his works. This retribution consists in entrance into the
happiness of heaven, immediately or after an appropriate purification, or entry into the eternal damnation of hell.

209. What is meant by the term "heaven"?

1023-1026   By "heaven" is meant the state of supreme and definitive happi-
1053   ness. Those who die in the grace of God and have no need of further
purification are gathered around Jesus and Mary, the angels and the
saints. They thus form the Church of heaven, where they see God
"face to face" (1 Corinthians 13:12). They live in a communion of love
with the Most Blessed Trinity and they intercede for us.

> *"True and subsistent life consists in this: the Father, through the
> Son and in the Holy Spirit, pouring out his heavenly gifts on all
> things without exception. Thanks to his mercy, we too, men that
> we are, have received the inalienable promise of eternal life."*
> (Saint Cyril of Jerusalem)

210. What is purgatory?

1030-1031   Purgatory is the state of those who die in God's friendship, assured of
1054   their eternal salvation, but who still have need of purification to enter
into the happiness of heaven.

211. How can we help the souls being purified in purgatory?

1032   Because of the communion of saints, the faithful who are still pilgrims on earth are able to help the souls in purgatory by offering
prayers in suffrage for them, especially the Eucharistic sacrifice. They
also help them by almsgiving, indulgences, and works of penance.

212. In what does hell consist?

1033-1035   Hell consists in the eternal damnation of those who die in mortal
1056-1057   sin through their own free choice. The principal suffering of hell is
eternal separation from God in whom alone we can have the life and
happiness for which we were created and for which we long. Christ
proclaimed this reality with the words, "Depart from me, you cursed,
into the eternal fire" (Matthew 25:41).

213. How can one reconcile the existence of hell with the infinite goodness of God?

1036-1037   God, while desiring "all to come to repentance" (2 Peter 3:9), neverthe-
less has created the human person to be free and responsible; and he

respects our decisions. Therefore, it is the human person who freely excludes himself from communion with God if at the moment of death he persists in mortal sin and refuses the merciful love of God.

214. In what does the final judgment consist?

The final or universal judgment consists in a sentence of happiness or eternal condemnation, which the Lord Jesus will issue in regard to the "just and the unjust" (Acts 24:15) when he returns as the Judge of the living and the dead. After the last judgment, the resurrected body will share in the retribution which the soul received at the particular judgment.

1038-1041
1058-1059

215. When will this judgment occur?

This judgment will come at the end of the world and only God knows the day and the hour.

1040

216. What is the hope of the new heavens and the new earth?

After the final judgment the universe itself, freed from its bondage to decay, will share in the glory of Christ with the beginning of "the new heavens" and a "new earth" (2 Peter 3:13). Thus, the fullness of the Kingdom of God will come about, that is to say, the definitive realization of the salvific plan of God to "unite all things in him, things in heaven and things on earth" (Ephesians 1:10). God will then be "all in all" (1 Corinthians 15:28) in eternal life.

1042-1050
1060

"AMEN"

217. What is the meaning of the word "Amen" with which we conclude our profession of faith?

The Hebrew word "Amen," which also concludes the last book of Sacred Scripture, some of the prayers of the New Testament, and the liturgical prayers of the Church, expresses our confident and total "yes" to what we professed in the Creed, entrusting ourselves completely to him who is the definitive "Amen" (Revelation 3:14; emphasis added), Christ the Lord.

1064-1065

In the painting displayed here, Jesus approaches his Apostles at table and gives them Communion one by one. This is a genre of painting which evidences the great reverence of the Church for the Eucharist through the centuries.

"Without the Lord's day, we cannot live," the martyr Emeritus said at the beginning of the fourth century during one of the most savage persecutions of the Christians, that of Diocletian in A.D. 304. Accused of having participated in the Eucharist with his community, he admitted without reservation: "Without the Eucharist we cannot live." And one of the martyrs added: "Yes, I went to the gathering and I celebrated the Supper of the Lord with my brothers because I am a Christian" (*Acts of the Martyrs of Abitene*, chapter 11 and 7, 16). For their fidelity to the Eucharist, the forty-nine North African martyrs were condemned to death. The Eucharistic Lord was the true life for Saturninus and his companion martyrs of Abitene in proconsular Africa. They preferred to die rather than be deprived of the Food of the Eucharist, the Bread of eternal life.

Saint Thomas Aquinas was accustomed at midday to enter the Church and place his forehead against the tabernacle with trust and surrender for an intimate and personal conversation with the Eucharistic Lord. This great theologian of the Middle Ages is also known for having composed the office for the feast of the Body of the Lord in which he set forth all his profound devotion for the Eucharist.

In the hymn for Morning Prayer (*Verbum supernum prodiens*), there is found a synthesis of the Catholic spirituality of the Eucharist:

"When he was about to be delivered over to death by the traitor and his accomplices, Jesus gave himself as the food of life to his disciples. To them he gave his Body and Blood under a twofold sign so that he could feed with a twofold substance the whole of man. By his birth he was given to us as a companion; by his seat at the table together with his chosen band, he was given to us as food; by his death he was given to us as our reward."

Aquinas, who called the Eucharist "the summit and perfection of all the spiritual life," could not but express the consciousness of the Church's faith for she believes in the Eucharist as the living presence of Jesus among us and as the indispensable nourishment for the spiritual life. The Eucharist is the golden thread that, beginning with the Last Supper, binds together all the ages of the Church's history up to ourselves today. The words of consecration, "This is my Body" and "This is my Blood" have been said at all times and places, even in the gulags, in the concentration camps, and in the thousands of prisons that are still here today. And it is upon this Eucharistic ground that the Church bases her life, her communion, and her mission.

Joos van Wassenhove, *Jesus Gives Communion to the Apostles*, National Gallery of the Marches, Urbino. (Used with permission.)

PART TWO
THE CELEBRATION OF THE CHRISTIAN MYSTERY

SECTION ONE
THE SACRAMENTAL ECONOMY

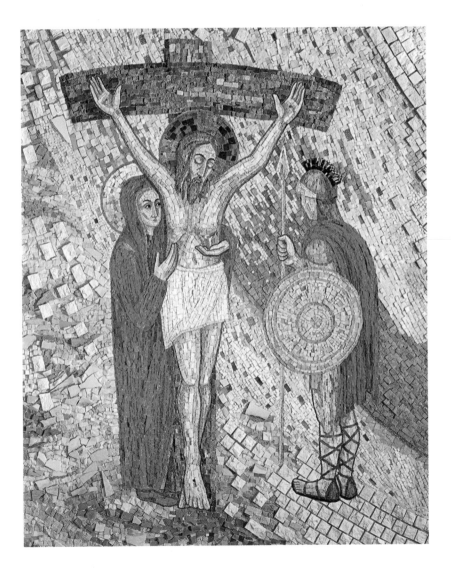

The sacrifice of the cross is the fount of the sacramental economy of the Church. In this image Mary, who is a figure for the Church, gathers in her left hand the blood and water which flow from the open side of Christ and which are symbols of the Church's sacraments.

"But when they came to Jesus and saw that he was already dead, they did not break his legs, but one soldier thrust his lance into his side, and immediately blood and water flowed out" (John 19:33-34).

Saint Augustine made this commentary:

"Christ our Lord, who in his suffering offered for us what in his being born he took from us and who has become in eternity the greatest of priests, has commanded that this sacrifice which you see be offered, that is, his body and blood. Indeed, his body, rent by the lance, poured out water and blood by which he forgave our sins. Remembering this grace and working out your salvation (which is God then working in you), draw near and become a partaker of this altar with fear and trembling. See in this bread that very body which hung upon the cross and in this cup that very blood which gushed from his side. Even the ancient sacrifices of God's People prefigured in their manifold kinds this unique sacrifice that was to come. Christ is at the same time the lamb by reason of the innocence of his pure soul and the goat by reason of his flesh which was in the likeness of sinful flesh. Any other thing which in many and various ways might be prefigured in the sacrifices of the Old Testament points solely to this sacrifice which has been revealed in the New Testament.

"Take then and eat the body of Christ since now you have become members of Christ in the body of Christ. Take and drink the blood of Christ. So as not to be cut off, eat that which unites you; so as not to think little of yourself, drink what is the price of your person. As this food, when you eat and drink of it, is transformed into yourself, so also do you transform yourselves into the body of Christ if you live in obedience and devotion to him. He indeed, when his passion was near, celebrated the Passover meal with his disciples. Taking the bread, he blessed it saying: *This is my body which will be given up for you.* In the same way, after having blessed it, he gave the cup saying: *This is my blood of the new covenant which will be shed for all for the forgiveness of sins.* This you have already read and heard of in the Gospel but you did not know that this Eucharist is the Son himself. Now with heart purified in an unstained conscience and with your body bathed in clean water, *look to him and you will be radiant with joy and your faces will not blush with shame*" (*Discourse*, 228B).

Chapel of the "Mother of the Redeemer," *Mosaic on the Wall of the Incarnation,* Vatican City. (Copyright © 1999, Ivan Rupnik/Libreria Editrice Vaticana.)

218. What is the liturgy?

The liturgy is the celebration of the mystery of Christ and in particu- 1066-1070
lar his Paschal Mystery. Through the exercise of the priestly office
of Jesus Christ the liturgy manifests in signs and brings about the
sanctification of humankind. The public worship which is due to God
is offered by the Mystical Body of Christ, that is, by its head and by
its members.

219. What place does the liturgy occupy in the life of the Church?

The liturgy as the sacred action *par excellence* is the summit toward 1071-1075
which the activity of the Church is directed and it is likewise the font
from which all her power flows. Through the liturgy Christ continues
the work of our redemption in, with and through his Church.

220. In what does the sacramental economy consist?

The sacramental economy consists in the communication of the fruits 1076
of Christ's redemption through the celebration of the sacraments
of the Church, most especially that of the Eucharist, "until he comes"
(1 Corinthians 11:26).

CHAPTER ONE
The Paschal Mystery in the Age of the Church

The Liturgy—Work of the Most Holy Trinity

221. In what way is the Father the source and the goal of the liturgy?

Through the liturgy the Father fills us with his blessings in the Word 1077-1083
made flesh who died and rose for us and pours into our hearts the 1110
Holy Spirit. At the same time, the Church blesses the Father by her
worship, praise, and thanksgiving and begs him for the gift of his Son
and the Holy Spirit.

222. What is the work of Christ in the liturgy?

1084-1090   In the liturgy of the Church, it is his own Paschal Mystery that Christ signifies and makes present. By giving the Holy Spirit to his Apostles he entrusted to them and their successors the power to make present the work of salvation through the Eucharistic sacrifice and the sacraments, in which he himself acts to communicate his grace to the faithful of all times and places throughout the world.

223. How does the Holy Spirit work in the liturgy of the Church?

1091-1109   The very closest cooperation is at work in the liturgy between the
1112   Holy Spirit and the Church. The Holy Spirit prepares the Church to encounter her Lord. He recalls and manifests Christ to the faith of the assembly. He makes the mystery of Christ really present. He unites the Church to the life and mission of Christ and makes the gift of communion bear fruit in the Church.

THE PASCHAL MYSTERY IN THE SACRAMENTS OF
THE CHURCH

224. What are the sacraments and which are they?

1113-1131   The sacraments, instituted by Christ and entrusted to the Church, are efficacious signs of grace perceptible to the senses. Through them divine life is bestowed upon us. There are seven sacraments: Baptism, Confirmation, Holy Eucharist, Penance, Anointing of the Sick, Holy Orders, and Matrimony.

225. What is the relationship of the sacraments to Christ?

1114-1116   The mysteries of Christ's life are the foundations of what he would henceforth dispense in the sacraments, through the ministers of his Church.

> "What was visible in our Savior has passed over into his mysteries." (Saint Leo the Great)

226. What is the link between the sacraments and the Church?

1117-1119   Christ has entrusted the sacraments to his Church. They are the sacraments "of the Church" in a twofold sense: they are "from her" insofar as they are actions of the Church which is the sacrament of Christ's action; and they are "for her" in as much as they build up the Church.

227. What is the *sacramental* character?

It is a spiritual *"seal"* bestowed by the sacraments of Baptism, Confirmation, and Holy Orders. It is a promise and guarantee of divine protection. By virtue of this seal the Christian is configured to Christ, participates in a variety of ways in his priesthood and takes his part in the Church according to different states and functions. He is, therefore, set apart for divine worship and the service of the Church. Because this character is indelible the sacraments that impress it on the soul are received only once in life.

1121

228. What is the relationship between the sacraments and faith?

The sacraments not only presuppose faith but with words and ritual elements they nourish, strengthen, and express it. By celebrating the sacraments, the Church professes the faith that comes from the Apostles. This explains the origin of the ancient saying, *"lex orandi, lex credendi,"* that is, the Church believes as she prays.

1122-1126 1133

229. Why are the sacraments efficacious?

The sacraments are efficacious *ex opere operato* ("by the very fact that the sacramental action is performed") because it is Christ who acts in the sacraments and communicates the grace they signify. The efficacy of the sacraments does not depend upon the personal holiness of the minister. However, the fruits of the sacraments do depend on the dispositions of the one who receives them.

1127-1128 1131

230. For what reason are the sacraments necessary for salvation?

For believers in Christ the sacraments, even if they are not all given to each of the faithful, are necessary for salvation because they confer sacramental grace, forgiveness of sins, adoption as children of God, conformation to Christ the Lord and membership in the Church. The Holy Spirit heals and transforms those who receive the sacraments.

1129

231. What is sacramental grace?

1129, 1131 Sacramental grace is the grace of the Holy Spirit which is given by
1134, 2003 Christ and is proper to each sacrament. This grace helps the faithful
in their journey toward holiness and so assists the Church as well to
grow in charity and in her witness to the world.

232. What is the relationship between the sacraments and everlasting life?

1130 In the sacraments the Church already receives a foretaste of eternal
life, while "awaiting our blessed hope, the appearing of the glory of
our great God and Savior Jesus Christ" (Titus 2:13).

CHAPTER TWO
The Sacramental Celebration of The Paschal Mystery

CELEBRATING THE LITURGY OF THE CHURCH

Who Celebrates?

233. Who acts in the liturgy?

1135-1137 In the liturgy it is the *whole Christ* (*Christus Totus*) who acts, Head and
1187 Body. As our High Priest he celebrates with his body, which is the
Church in heaven and on earth.

234. Who celebrates the heavenly liturgy?

1138-1139 The heavenly liturgy is celebrated by the angels, by the saints of
the Old and New Testament, particularly the Mother of God, by the
Apostles, by the martyrs, and by the "great multitude, which no one
could count, from every nation, race, people, and tongue" (Revelation
7:9). When we celebrate the mystery of our salvation in the sacraments
we participate in this eternal liturgy.

235. How does the Church on earth celebrate the liturgy?

The Church on earth celebrates the liturgy as a priestly people in which each one acts according to his proper function in the unity of the Holy Spirit. The baptized offer themselves in a spiritual sacrifice; the ordained ministers celebrate according to the Order they received for the service of all the members of the Church; the bishops and priests act in the Person of Christ the Head.

1140-1144
1188

How Is the Liturgy Celebrated?

236. How is the liturgy celebrated?

The celebration of the liturgy is interwoven with signs and symbols whose meaning is rooted in creation and in human culture. It is determined by the events of the Old Testament and is fully revealed in the Person and work of Christ.

1145

237. From where do the sacramental signs come?

Some come from created things (light, water, fire, bread, wine, oil); others come from social life (washing, anointing, breaking of bread). Still others come from the history of salvation in the Old Covenant (the Passover rites, the sacrifices, the laying on of hands, the consecrations). These signs, some of which are normative and unchangeable, were taken up by Christ and are made the bearers of his saving and sanctifying action.

1146-1152
1189

238. What is the link between the actions and the words in the celebration of the sacraments?

Actions and words are very closely linked in the celebration of the sacraments. Indeed, even if the symbolic actions are already in themselves a language, it is necessary that the words of the rite accompany and give life to these actions. The liturgical words and actions are inseparable both insofar as they are meaningful signs and insofar as they bring about what they signify.

1153-1155
1190

239. What are the criteria for the proper use of singing and music in liturgical celebrations?

1156-1158
1191

Since song and music are closely connected with liturgical action they must respect the following criteria. They should conform to Catholic doctrine in their texts, drawn preferably from Sacred Scripture and liturgical sources. They should be a beautiful expression of prayer. The music should be of a high quality. Song and music should encourage the participation of the liturgical assembly. They should express the cultural richness of the People of God and the sacred and solemn character of the celebration. "He who sings, prays twice" (Saint Augustine).

240. What is the purpose of holy images?

1159-1161
1192

The image of Christ is the liturgical icon *par excellence*. Other images, representations of Our Lady and of the Saints, signify Christ who is glorified in them. They proclaim the same Gospel message that Sacred Scripture communicates by the word and they help to awaken and nourish the faith of believers.

When Is the Liturgy Celebrated?

241. What is the center of the liturgical season?

1163-1167
1193

The center of the liturgical season is Sunday which is the foundation and kernel of the entire liturgical year and has its culmination in the annual celebration of Easter, the feast of feasts.

242. What is the function of the liturgical year?

1168-1173
1194-1195

In the liturgical year the Church celebrates the whole mystery of Christ from his Incarnation to his return in glory. On set days the Church venerates with special love the Blessed Virgin Mary, the Mother of God. The Church also keeps the memorials of saints who lived for Christ, who suffered with him, and who live with him in glory.

243. What is the Liturgy of the Hours?

1174-1178
1196

The Liturgy of the Hours, which is the public and common prayer of the Church, is the prayer of Christ with his body, the Church.

Through the Liturgy of the Hours the mystery of Christ, which we celebrate in the Eucharist, sanctifies and transforms the whole of each day. It is composed mainly of psalms, other biblical texts, and readings from the Fathers and spiritual masters.

Where Is the Liturgy Celebrated?

244. Does the Church need places in order to celebrate the liturgy?

The worship "in spirit and truth" (John 4:24) of the New Covenant is not tied exclusively to any place because Christ is the true temple of God. Through him Christians and the whole Church become temples of the living God by the action of the Holy Spirit. Nonetheless, the people of God in their earthly condition need places in which the community can gather to celebrate the liturgy.   1179-1181 1197-1198

245. What are sacred buildings?

They are the houses of God, a symbol of the Church that lives in that place as well as of the heavenly Jerusalem. Above all they are places of prayer in which the Church celebrates the Eucharist and worships Christ who is truly present in the tabernacle.   1181 1198-1199

246. What are the privileged places inside sacred buildings?

They are: the altar, the tabernacle, the place where the sacred Chrism and other holy oils are kept, the chair of the bishop (cathedra) or the chair of the priest, the ambo, the baptismal font, and the confessional.   1182-1186

LITURGICAL DIVERSITY AND THE UNITY OF THE MYSTERY

247. Why is the one Mystery of Christ celebrated by the Church according to various liturgical traditions?

The answer is that the unfathomable richness of the mystery of Christ cannot be exhausted by any single liturgical tradition. From the very beginning, therefore, this richness found expression among various   1200-1204 1207-1209 peoples and cultures in ways that are characterized by a wonderful diversity and complementarity.

248. What is the criterion that assures unity in the midst of plurality?

1209   It is fidelity to the Apostolic Tradition, that is, the communion in the faith and in the sacraments received from the Apostles, a communion that is both signified and guaranteed by apostolic succession. The Church is Catholic and therefore can integrate into her unity all the authentic riches of cultures.

249. Is everything immutable in the liturgy?

1205-1206   In the liturgy, particularly in that of the sacraments, there are unchangeable elements because they are of divine institution. The Church is the faithful guardian of them. There are also, however, elements subject to change which the Church has the power and on occasion also the duty to adapt to the cultures of diverse peoples.

SECTION TWO
THE SEVEN SACRAMENTS
OF THE CHURCH

The seven sacraments are

Baptism

Confirmation

Holy Eucharist

Penance

Anointing of the Sick

Holy Orders

Matrimony

The sacraments of the Church are the fruit of the redemptive sacrifice of Jesus on the cross. The triptych portrays a church in which the seven sacraments are celebrated. At the center the cross is raised in a predominant way. At the feet of the Crucified, there is Mary, heartbroken, supported by John and the holy women. In the back a priest celebrating Mass elevates the Host after the consecration to show that the sacrifice of the cross is made present again in the Eucharistic celebration under the forms of bread and wine.

In the square to the left (p. 75) which shows a side chapel, the sacraments of Baptism, Confirmation, administered by the bishop, and Penance are portrayed. The one on the right (p. 76) depicts the sacraments of Holy Orders, again administered by the bishop, Matrimony, and Anointing of the Sick.

Rogier Van Der Weyden, *Triptych of the Seven Sacraments*, Koninklijk Museum of the Fine Arts, Anversa. (Photo credit: Erich Lessing/Art Resource, NY.)

250. How are the sacraments of the Church divided?

The sacraments are divided into: the sacraments of Christian initia- 1210-1211
tion (Baptism, Confirmation, and Holy Eucharist); the sacraments of
healing (Penance and Anointing of the Sick); and the sacraments at
the service of communion and mission (Holy Orders and Matrimony).
The sacraments touch all the important moments of Christian life. All
of the sacraments are ordered to the Holy Eucharist "as to their end"
(Saint Thomas Aquinas).

CHAPTER ONE
The Sacraments of Christian Initiation

251. How is Christian initiation brought about?

Christian initiation is accomplished by means of the sacraments 1212
which establish the *foundations* of Christian life. The faithful born 1275
anew by Baptism are strengthened by Confirmation and are then
nourished by the Eucharist.

THE SACRAMENT OF BAPTISM

252. What names are given to the first sacrament of initiation?

This sacrament is primarily called *Baptism* because of the central rite 1213-1216
with which it is celebrated. To baptize means to "immerse" in water. 1276-1277
The one who is baptized is immersed into the death of Christ and
rises with him as a "new creature" (2 Corinthians 5:17). This sacrament is also called the "bath of regeneration and renewal in the Holy
Spirit" (Titus 3:5); and it is called "enlightenment" because the baptized becomes "a son of light" (Ephesians 5:8).

253. How is Baptism prefigured in the Old Covenant?

In the Old Covenant Baptism was pre-figured in various ways: *water,* 1217-1222
seen as source of life and of death; in *the Ark of Noah,* which saved by
means of water; in *the passing through the Red Sea,* which liberated Israel
from Egyptian slavery; in *the crossing of the Jordan River,* that brought
Israel into the promised land which is the image of eternal life.

254. Who brought to fulfillment those prefigurations?

1223-1224   All the Old Covenant prefigurations find their fulfillment in Jesus Christ. At the beginning of his public life Jesus had himself baptized by John the Baptist in the Jordan. On the cross, blood and water, signs of Baptism and the Eucharist, flowed from his pierced side. After his Resurrection he gave to his Apostles this mission: "Go therefore and make disciples of all nations, baptizing them in the name of the Father and of the Son and of the Holy Spirit" (Matthew 28:19).

255. Starting when and to whom has the Church administered Baptism?

1226-1228   From the day of Pentecost, the Church has administered Baptism to anyone who believes in Jesus Christ.

256. In what does the essential rite of Baptism consist?

1229-1245   The essential rite of this sacrament consists in immersing the candi-
1278   date in water or pouring water over his or her head while invoking the name of the Father and the Son and the Holy Spirit.

257. Who can receive Baptism?

1246-1252   Every person not yet baptized is able to receive Baptism.

258. Why does the Church baptize infants?

1250   The Church baptizes infants because they are born with original sin. They need to be freed from the power of the Evil One and brought into that realm of freedom which belongs to the children of God.

259. What is required of one who is to be baptized?

1253-1255   Everyone who is to be baptized is required to make a profession of faith. This is done personally in the case of an adult or by the parents and by the Church in the case of infants. Also the godfather or the godmother and the whole ecclesial community share the responsibility for baptismal preparation (catechumenate) as well as for the development and safeguarding of the faith and grace given at baptism.

260. Who can baptize?

The ordinary ministers of Baptism are the bishop and the priest. In   1256
the Latin Church the deacon also can baptize. In case of necessity any   1284
person can baptize provided he has the intention of doing what the
Church does. This is done by pouring water on the head of the candidate while saying the Trinitarian formula for Baptism: "I baptize
you in the name of the Father and of the Son and of the Holy Spirit."

261. Is Baptism necessary for salvation?

Baptism is necessary for salvation for all those to whom the Gospel   1257
has been proclaimed and who have had the possibility of asking for
this sacrament.

262. Is it possible to be saved without Baptism?

Since Christ died for the salvation of all, those can be saved with-   1258-1261
out Baptism who die for the faith (*Baptism of blood*). Catechumens   1281-1283
and all those who, even without knowing Christ and the Church,
still (under the impulse of grace) sincerely seek God and strive to
do his will can also be saved without Baptism (*Baptism of desire*). The
Church in her liturgy entrusts children who die without Baptism to
the mercy of God.

263. What are the effects of Baptism?

Baptism takes away original sin, all personal sins and all punishment   1262-1274
due to sin. It makes the baptized person a participant in the divine   1279-1280
life of the Trinity through sanctifying grace, the grace of justification
which incorporates one into Christ and into his Church. It gives one
a share in the priesthood of Christ and provides the basis for communion with all Christians. It bestows the theological virtues and the
gifts of the Holy Spirit. A baptized person belongs forever to Christ.
He is marked with the indelible seal of Christ (*character*).

264. What is the meaning of the Christian name received at Baptism?

The name is important because God knows each of us by name, that   2156-2159
is, in our uniqueness as persons. In Baptism a Christian receives his   2167
or her own name in the Church. It should preferably be the name of a

saint who might offer the baptized a model of sanctity and an assurance of his or her intercession before God.

The Sacrament of Confirmation

265. What place does Confirmation have in the divine plan of salvation?

1285-1288 In the Old Testament the prophets announced that the Spirit of the
1315 Lord would rest on the awaited Messiah and on the entire messianic people. The whole life and mission of Jesus were carried out in total communion with the Holy Spirit. The Apostles received the Holy Spirit at Pentecost and proclaimed "the mighty works of God" (Acts 2:11). They gave the gift of the same Spirit to the newly baptized by the laying on of hands. Down through the centuries, the Church has continued to live by the Spirit and to impart him to her children.

266. Why is this sacrament called *Chrismation* or *Confirmation*?

1289 It is called *Chrismation* (in the Eastern Churches: anointing with holy myron or chrism) because the essential rite of the sacrament is anointing with chrism. It is called *Confirmation* because it confirms and strengthens baptismal grace.

267. What is the essential rite of Confirmation?

1290-1301 The essential rite of Confirmation is the anointing with Sacred Chrism
1318 (oil mixed with balsam and consecrated by the bishop), which is done
1320-1321 by the laying on of the hand of the minister who pronounces the sacramental words proper to the rite. In the West this anointing is done on the forehead of the baptized with the words, "Be sealed with the Gift of the Holy Spirit." In the Eastern Churches of the Byzantine rite this anointing is also done on other parts of the body with the words, "The seal of the Gift of the Holy Spirit."

268. What is the effect of Confirmation?

1302-1305 The effect of Confirmation is a special outpouring of the Holy Spirit
1316-1317 like that of Pentecost. This outpouring impresses on the soul an indelible character and produces a growth in the grace of Baptism. It roots the recipient more deeply in divine sonship, binds him more

firmly to Christ and to the Church and reinvigorates the gifts of the Holy Spirit in his soul. It gives a special strength to witness to the Christian faith.

269. Who can receive this sacrament?

Only those already baptized can and should receive this sacrament which can be received only once. To receive Confirmation efficaciously the candidate must be in the state of grace. 1306-1311 1319

270. Who is the minister of Confirmation?

The original minister of Confirmation is the bishop. In this way the link between the confirmed and the Church in her apostolic dimension is made manifest. When a priest confers this sacrament, as ordinarily happens in the East and in special cases in the West, the link with the bishop and with the Church is expressed by the priest who is the collaborator of the bishop and by the Sacred Chrism, consecrated by the bishop himself. 1312-1314

THE SACRAMENT OF THE EUCHARIST

271. What is the Eucharist?

The Eucharist is the very sacrifice of the Body and Blood of the Lord Jesus which he instituted to perpetuate the sacrifice of the cross throughout the ages until his return in glory. Thus he entrusted to his Church this memorial of his death and Resurrection. It is a sign of unity, a bond of charity, a paschal banquet, in which Christ is consumed, the mind is filled with grace, and a pledge of future glory is given to us. 1322-1323 1409

272. When did Jesus Christ institute the Eucharist?

Jesus instituted the Eucharist on Holy Thursday "the night when he was betrayed" (1 Corinthians 11:23), as he celebrated the Last Supper with his Apostles. 1323 1337-1340

273. How did he institute the Eucharist?

1337-1340   After he had gathered with his apostles in the Cenacle, Jesus took
1365, 1406   bread in his hands. He broke it and gave it to them saying, "Take this,
all of you, and eat of it, for this is my Body, which will be given up
for you." Then, he took the cup of wine in his hands and said, "Take
this, all of you, and drink from it, for this is the chalice of my Blood,
the Blood of the new and eternal covenant, which will be poured out
for you and for many for the forgiveness of sins. Do this in memory
of me" (*Roman Missal*, EP I, 89-90).

274. What does the Eucharist represent in the life of the Church?

1324-1327   It is the source and summit of all Christian life. In the Eucharist, the
1407   sanctifying action of God in our regard and our worship of him reach
their high point. It contains the whole spiritual good of the Church,
Christ himself, our Pasch. Communion with divine life and the unity
of the People of God are both expressed and effected by the Eucharist.
Through the eucharistic celebration we are united already with the
liturgy of heaven and we have a foretaste of eternal life.

275. What are the names for this sacrament?

1328-1332   The unfathomable richness of this sacrament is expressed in different names which evoke its various aspects. The most common names
are: the Eucharist, Holy Mass, the Lord's Supper, the Breaking of
the Bread, the Eucharistic Celebration, the Memorial of the Passion,
Death and Resurrection of the Lord, the Holy Sacrifice, the Holy and
Divine Liturgy, the Sacred Mysteries, the Most Holy Sacrament of the
Altar, and Holy Communion.

276. Where does the Eucharist fit in the divine plan of salvation?

1333-1344   The Eucharist was foreshadowed in the Old Covenant above all in the
annual Passover meal celebrated every year by the Jews with unleav-
ened bread to commemorate their hasty, liberating departure from
Egypt. Jesus foretold it in his teaching and he instituted it when he
celebrated the Last Supper with his Apostles in a Passover meal. The
Church, faithful to the command of her Lord, "Do this in memory of
me" (1 Corinthians 11:24), has always celebrated the Eucharist, especially on Sunday, the day of the Resurrection of Jesus.

277. How is the celebration of the Holy Eucharist carried out?

The Eucharist unfolds in two great parts which together form one, single, single act of worship. The Liturgy of the Word involves proclaiming and listening to the Word of God. The Liturgy of the Eucharist includes the presentation of the bread and wine, the prayer or the anaphora containing the words of consecration, and communion.

1345-1355
1408

278. Who is the minister for the celebration of the Eucharist?

The celebrant of the Eucharist is a validly ordained priest (bishop or priest) who acts in the Person of Christ the Head and in the name of the Church.

1348
1411

279. What are the essential and necessary elements for celebrating the Eucharist?

The essential elements are wheat bread and grape wine.

1412

280. In what way is the Eucharist a *memorial* of the sacrifice of Christ?

The Eucharist is a *memorial* in the sense that it makes present and actual the sacrifice which Christ offered to the Father on the cross, once and for all on behalf of mankind. The sacrificial character of the Holy Eucharist is manifested in the very words of institution, "This is my body which is given for you" and "This cup is the New Covenant in my Blood that will be shed for you" (Luke 22:19-20). The sacrifice of the cross and the sacrifice of the Eucharist are *one and the same sacrifice*. The priest and the victim are the same; only the manner of offering is different: in a bloody manner on the cross, in an unbloody manner in the Eucharist.

1362-1367

281. In what way does the Church participate in the eucharistic sacrifice?

In the Eucharist the sacrifice of Christ becomes also the sacrifice of the members of his body. The lives of the faithful, their praise, their suffering, their prayers, their work, are united to those of Christ. In as much as it is a sacrifice, the Eucharist is likewise offered for all the faithful, living and dead, in reparation for the sins of all and to obtain

1368-1372
1414

spiritual and temporal benefits from God. The Church in heaven is also united to the offering of Christ.

282. How is Christ present in the Eucharist?

1373-1375
1413
Jesus Christ is present in the Eucharist in a unique and incomparable way. He is present in a true, real and substantial way, with his Body and his Blood, with his Soul and his Divinity. In the Eucharist, therefore, there is present in a sacramental way, that is, under the Eucharistic species of bread and wine, Christ whole and entire, God and Man.

283. What is the meaning of *transubstantiation*?

1376-1377
1413
Transubstantiation means the change of the whole substance of bread into the substance of the Body of Christ and of the whole substance of wine into the substance of his Blood. This change is brought about in the eucharistic prayer through the efficacy of the word of Christ and by the action of the Holy Spirit. However, the outward characteristics of bread and wine, that is, the "eucharistic species," remain unaltered.

284. Does the breaking of the bread divide Christ?

1377
The breaking of the bread does not divide Christ. He is present whole and entire in each of the eucharistic species and in each of their parts.

285. How long does the presence of Christ last in the Eucharist?

1377
The presence of Christ continues in the Eucharist as long as the eucharistic species subsist.

286. What kind of worship is due to the sacrament of the Eucharist?

1378-1381
1418
The worship due to the sacrament of the Eucharist, whether during the celebration of the Mass or outside it, is the worship of *latria*, that is, the adoration given to God alone. The Church guards with the greatest care Hosts that have been consecrated. She brings them to the sick and to other persons who find it impossible to participate at Mass. She also presents them for the solemn adoration of the faithful

and she bears them in processions. The Church encourages the faithful to make frequent visits to adore the Blessed Sacrament reserved in the tabernacle.

287. Why is the Holy Eucharist the paschal banquet?

The Holy Eucharist is the paschal banquet in as much as Christ sacramentally makes present his Passover and gives us his Body and Blood, offered as food and drink, uniting us to himself and to one another in his sacrifice.

1382-1384
1391-1396

288. What is the meaning of the altar?

The *altar* is the symbol of Christ himself who is present both as sacrificial victim (the altar of the sacrifice) and as food from heaven which is given to us (the table of the Lord).

1383
1410

289. When does the Church oblige her members to participate at Holy Mass?

The Church obliges the faithful to participate at Holy Mass every Sunday and on holy days of obligation. She recommends participation at Holy Mass on other days as well.

1389
1417

290. When must one receive Holy Communion?

The Church recommends that the faithful, if they have the required dispositions, receive Holy Communion whenever they participate at Holy Mass. However, the Church obliges them to receive Holy Communion at least once a year during the Easter season.

1389

291. What is required to receive Holy Communion?

To receive Holy Communion one must be fully incorporated into the Catholic Church and be in the state of grace, that is, not conscious of being in mortal sin. Anyone who is conscious of having committed a grave sin must first receive the sacrament of Reconciliation before going to Communion. Also important for those receiving Holy Communion are a spirit of recollection and prayer, observance of the fast prescribed by the Church, and an appropriate disposition of the body (gestures and dress) as a sign of respect for Christ.

1385-1389
1415

292. What are the fruits of Holy Communion?

1391-1397   Holy Communion increases our union with Christ and with his
1416   Church. It preserves and renews the life of grace received at Baptism
            and Confirmation and makes us grow in love for our neighbor. It
            strengthens us in charity, wipes away venial sins and preserves us
            from mortal sin in the future.

293. When is it possible to give Holy Communion to other Christians?

1398-1401   Catholic ministers may give Holy Communion licitly to members
            of the Oriental Churches which are not in full communion with the
            Catholic Church whenever they ask for it of their own will and pos-
            sess the required dispositions. Catholic ministers may licitly give
            Holy Communion to members of other ecclesial communities only
            if, in grave necessity, they ask for it of their own will, possess the
            required dispositions, and give evidence of holding the Catholic faith
            regarding the sacrament.

294. Why is the Eucharist a "pledge of future glory"?

1402-1405   The Eucharist is a pledge of future glory because it fills us with every
            grace and heavenly blessing. It fortifies us for our pilgrimage in this
            life and makes us long for eternal life. It unites us already to Christ
            seated at the right hand of the Father, to the Church in heaven and to
            the Blessed Virgin and all the saints.

> *In the Eucharist, we "break the one bread that provides the medi-*
> *cine of immortality, the antidote for death and the food that makes*
> *us live forever in Jesus Christ."* (Saint Ignatius of Antioch)

CHAPTER TWO
The Sacraments of Healing

295. Why did Christ institute the sacraments of Penance and the Anointing of the Sick?

Christ, the physician of our soul and body, instituted these sacraments because the new life that he gives us in the sacraments of Christian initiation can be weakened and even lost because of sin. Therefore, Christ willed that his Church should continue his work of healing and salvation by means of these two sacraments.   1420-1421 1426

THE SACRAMENT OF PENANCE AND RECONCILIATION

296. What is the name of this sacrament?

It is called the sacrament of Penance, the sacrament of Reconciliation, the sacrament of Forgiveness, the sacrament of Confession, and the sacrament of Conversion.   1422-1424

297. Why is there a sacrament of Reconciliation after Baptism?

Since the new life of grace received in Baptism does not abolish the weakness of human nature nor the inclination to sin (that is, *concupiscence*), Christ instituted this sacrament for the conversion of the baptized who have been separated from him by sin.   1425-1426 1484

298. When did he institute this sacrament?

The risen Lord instituted this sacrament on the evening of Easter when he showed himself to his Apostles and said to them, "Receive the Holy Spirit. If you forgive the sins of any, they are forgiven; if you retain the sins of any, they are retained" (John 20:22-23).   1485

299. Do the baptized have need of conversion?

The call of Christ to conversion continues to resound in the lives of the baptized. Conversion is a continuing obligation for the whole Church. She is holy but includes sinners in her midst.   1427-1429

300. What is interior penance?

1430-1433 It is the movement of a "contrite heart" (Psalm 51:17) drawn by divine
1490 grace to respond to the merciful love of God. This entails sorrow for
and abhorrence of sins committed, a firm purpose not to sin again
in the future and trust in the help of God. It is nourished by hope in
divine mercy.

301. What forms does penance take in the Christian life?

1434-1439 Penance can be expressed in many and various ways but above all in
fasting, prayer, and almsgiving. These and many other forms of penance can be practiced in the daily life of a Christian, particularly during the time of Lent and on the penitential day of Friday.

302. What are the essential elements of the sacrament of Reconciliation?

1440-1449 The essential elements are two: the acts of the penitent who comes to
repentance through the action of the Holy Spirit, and the absolution
of the priest who in the name of Christ grants forgiveness and determines the ways of making satisfaction.

303. What are the acts of the penitent?

1450-1460 They are: a careful *examination of conscience*; *contrition* (or repentance),
1487-1492 which is perfect when it is motivated by love of God and imperfect if
it rests on other motives and which includes the determination not to
sin again; *confession*, which consists in the telling of one's sins to the
priest; and *satisfaction* or the carrying out of certain acts of penance
which the confessor imposes upon the penitent to repair the damage
caused by sin.

304. Which sins must be confessed?

1456 All grave sins not yet confessed, which a careful examination of
conscience brings to mind, must be brought to the sacrament of
Penance. The confession of serious sins is the only ordinary way to
obtain forgiveness.

305. When is a person obliged to confess mortal sins?

Each of the faithful who has reached the age of discretion is bound to confess his or her mortal sins at least once a year and always before receiving Holy Communion.

1457

306. Why can venial sins also be the object of sacramental confession?

The confession of venial sins is strongly recommended by the Church, even if this is not strictly necessary, because it helps us to form a correct conscience and to fight against evil tendencies. It allows us to be healed by Christ and to progress in the life of the Spirit.

1458

307. Who is the minister of this sacrament?

Christ has entrusted the ministry of Reconciliation to his Apostles, to the bishops who are their successors and to the priests who are the collaborators of the bishops, all of whom become thereby instruments of the mercy and justice of God. They exercise their power of forgiving sins *in the name of the Father and of the Son and of the Holy Spirit.*

1461-1466
1495

308. To whom is the absolution of some sins reserved?

The absolution of certain particularly grave sins (like those punished by excommunication) is reserved to the Apostolic See or to the local bishop or to priests who are authorized by them. Any priest, however, can absolve a person who is in danger of death from any sin and excommunication.

1463

309. Is a confessor bound to secrecy?

Given the delicacy and greatness of this ministry and the respect due to people every confessor, without any exception and under very severe penalties, is bound to maintain "the sacramental seal" which means absolute secrecy about the sins revealed to him in confession.

1467

310. What are the effects of this sacrament?

The effects of the sacrament of Penance are: reconciliation with God and therefore the forgiveness of sins; reconciliation with the Church; recovery, if it has been lost, of the state of grace; remission of the

1468-1470
1496

eternal punishment merited by mortal sins, and remission, at least in part, of the temporal punishment which is the consequence of sin; peace, serenity of conscience and spiritual consolation; and an increase of spiritual strength for the struggle of Christian living.

311. Can this sacrament be celebrated in some cases with a general confession and general absolution?

1480-1484   In cases of serious necessity (as in imminent danger of death) recourse may be had to a communal celebration of Reconciliation with general confession and general absolution, as long as the norms of the Church are observed and there is the intention of individually confessing one's grave sins in due time.

312. What are indulgences?

1471-1479
1498   Indulgences are the remission before God of the temporal punishment due to sins whose guilt has already been forgiven. The faithful Christian who is duly disposed gains the indulgence under prescribed conditions for either himself or the departed. Indulgences are granted through the ministry of the Church which, as the dispenser of the grace of redemption, distributes the treasury of the merits of Christ and the saints.

THE SACRAMENT OF ANOINTING OF THE SICK

313. How was sickness viewed in the Old Testament?

1499-1502   In the Old Testament sickness was experienced as a sign of weakness and at the same time perceived as mysteriously bound up with sin. The prophets intuited that sickness could also have a redemptive value for one's own sins and those of others. Thus sickness was lived out in the presence of God from whom people implored healing.

314. What is the significance of Jesus' compassion for the sick?

1503-1505   The compassion of Jesus toward the sick and his many healings of the infirm were a clear sign that with him had come the Kingdom of God and therefore victory over sin, over suffering, and over death. By his own Passion and death he gave new meaning to our suffering which, when united with his own, can become a means of purification and of salvation for us and for others.

315. What is the attitude of the Church toward the sick?

Having received from the Lord the charge to heal the sick, the Church strives to carry it out by taking care of the sick and accompanying them with her prayer of intercession. Above all, the Church possesses a sacrament specifically intended for the benefit of the sick. This sacrament was instituted by Christ and is attested by Saint James: "Is anyone among you sick? Let him call in the presbyters of the Church and let them pray over him and anoint him with oil in the name of the Lord" (James 5:14-15). 1506-1513 1526-1527

316. Who can receive the sacrament of the anointing of the sick?

Any member of the faithful can receive this sacrament as soon as he or she begins to be in danger of death because of sickness or old age. The faithful who receive this sacrament can receive it several times if their illness becomes worse or another serious sickness afflicts them. The celebration of this sacrament should, if possible, be preceded by individual confession on the part of the sick person. 1514-1515 1528-1529

317. Who administers this sacrament?

This sacrament can be administered only by priests (bishops or presbyters). 1516 1530

318. How is this sacrament celebrated?

The celebration of this sacrament consists essentially in an *anointing* with oil which may be blessed by the bishop. The anointing is on the forehead and on the hands of the sick person (in the Roman rite) or also on other parts of the body (in the other rites) accompanied by the *prayer* of the priest who asks for the special grace of this sacrament. 1517-1519 1531

319. What are the effects of this sacrament?

This sacrament confers a special grace which unites the sick person more intimately to the Passion of Christ for his good and for the good of all the Church. It gives comfort, peace, courage, and even the forgiveness of sins if the sick person is not able to make a confession. 1520-1523 1532

Sometimes, if it is the will of God, this sacrament even brings about the restoration of physical health. In any case this Anointing prepares the sick person for the journey to the Father's house.

320. What is Viaticum?

1524-1525   Viaticum is the Holy Eucharist received by those who are about to leave this earthly life and are preparing for the journey to eternal life. Communion in the Body and Blood of Christ who died and rose from the dead, received at the moment of passing from this world to the Father, is the seed of eternal life and the power of the resurrection.

CHAPTER THREE

The Sacraments at the Service of Communion and Mission

321. What are the sacraments at the service of communion and mission?

1533-1535   Two sacraments, Holy Orders and Matrimony, confer a special grace for a particular mission in the Church to serve and build up the People of God. These sacraments contribute in a special way to ecclesial communion and to the salvation of others.

THE SACRAMENT OF HOLY ORDERS

322. What is the sacrament of Holy Orders?

1536   It is the sacrament through which the mission entrusted by Christ to his Apostles continues to be exercised in the Church until the end of time.

323. Why is this sacrament called Holy Orders?

1537-1538   *Orders* designates an ecclesial body into which one enters by means of a special consecration (ordination). Through a special gift of the Holy Spirit, this sacrament enables the ordained to exercise a *sacred power* in the name and with the authority of Christ for the service of the People of God.

324. What place does the sacrament of Holy Orders have in the divine plan of salvation?

This sacrament was prefigured in the Old Covenant in the service of the Levites, in the priesthood of Aaron, and in the institution of "the seventy elders" (Numbers 11:25). These prefigurations find their fulfillment in Christ Jesus who by the sacrifice of the cross is the "one mediator between God and men" (1 Timothy 2:5), the "High Priest according to the order of Melchizedek" (Hebrews 5:10). The one priesthood of Christ is made present in the ministerial priesthood. 1539-1546
1590-1591

> *"Only Christ is the true priest, the others being only his ministers."* (Saint Thomas Aquinas)

325. What are the degrees that make up the sacrament of Holy Orders?

The sacrament of Holy Orders is composed of three degrees which are irreplaceable for the organic structure of the Church: the episcopate, the presbyterate and the diaconate. 1554
1593

326. What is the effect of episcopal ordination?

Episcopal ordination confers the fullness of the sacrament of Holy Orders. It makes the bishop a legitimate successor of the Apostles and integrates him into the episcopal college to share with the Pope and the other bishops care for all the churches. It confers on him the offices of teaching, sanctifying, and ruling. 1557-1558
1594

327. What is the office confided to a bishop in a particular Church?

The bishop to whom the care of a particular Church is entrusted is the visible head and foundation of unity for that Church. For the sake of that Church, as vicar of Christ, he fulfills the office of shepherd and is assisted by his own priests and deacons. 1560-1561

328. What is the effect of ordination to the priesthood?

1562-1567 The anointing of the Spirit seals the priest with an indelible, spiritual
1595   character that configures him to Christ the priest and enables him
           to act in the name of Christ the Head. As a co-worker of the order of
           bishops he is consecrated to preach the Gospel, to celebrate divine
           worship, especially the Eucharist from which his ministry draws its
           strength, and to be a shepherd of the faithful.

329. How does a priest carry out his proper ministry?

1568 A priest, although ordained for a universal mission, exercises his
      ministry in a particular Church. This ministry is pursued in sacra-
      mental brotherhood with other priests who form the "presbyterate."
      In communion with the bishop, and depending upon him, they bear
      responsibility for the particular Church.

330. What is the effect of the ordination to the diaconate?

1569-1571 The deacon, configured to Christ the servant of all, is ordained for
1596   service to the Church. He carries out this service under the authority
           of his proper bishop by the ministry of the Word, of divine worship,
           of pastoral care and of charity.

331. How is the sacrament of Holy Orders celebrated?

1572-1574 The sacrament of Holy Orders is conferred, in each of its three degrees,
1597   by means of the *imposition of hands* on the head of the ordinand by the
           bishop who pronounces the solemn *prayer* of consecration. With this
           prayer he asks God on behalf of the ordinand for the special outpour-
           ing of the Holy Spirit and for the gifts of the Spirit proper to the min-
           istry to which he is being ordained.

332. Who can confer this sacrament?

1575-1576 Only validly ordained bishops, as successors of the Apostles, can con-
1600   fer the sacrament of Holy Orders.

333. Who can receive this sacrament?

1577-1578 This sacrament can only be validly received by a baptized man.
1598   The Church recognizes herself as bound by this choice made by the

Lord Himself. No one can demand to receive the sacrament of Holy Orders, but must be judged suitable for the ministry by the authorities of the Church.

334. Is it necessary to be celibate to receive the sacrament of Holy Orders?

It is always necessary to be celibate for the episcopacy. For the priesthood in the Latin Church men who are practicing Catholics and celibate are chosen, men who intend to continue to live a celibate life "for the kingdom of heaven" (Matthew 19:12). In the Eastern Churches marriage is not permitted after one has been ordained. Married men can be ordained to the permanent diaconate. 1579-1580 1599

335. What are the effects of the sacrament of Holy Orders?

This sacrament yields a special outpouring of the Holy Spirit which configures the recipient to Christ in his triple office as Priest, Prophet, and King, according to the respective degrees of the sacrament. Ordination confers an indelible spiritual character and therefore cannot be repeated or conferred for a limited time. 1581-1589

336. With what authority is the priestly ministry exercised?

Ordained priests in the exercise of their sacred ministry speak and act not on their own authority, nor even by mandate or delegation of the community, but rather in the Person of Christ the Head and in the name of the Church. Therefore, the ministerial priesthood differs essentially and not just in degree from the priesthood common to all the faithful for whose service Christ instituted it. 1547-1553 1592

THE SACRAMENT OF MATRIMONY

337. What is the plan of God regarding man and woman?

God who is love and who created man and woman for love has called them to love. By creating man and woman he called them to an intimate communion of life and of love in marriage: "So they are no longer two but one flesh" (Matthew 19:6). God said to them in blessing "Be fruitful and multiply" (Genesis 1:28). 1601-1605

338. For what ends has God instituted Matrimony?

1659-1660   The marital union of man and woman, which is founded and endowed with its own proper laws by the Creator, is by its very nature ordered to the communion and good of the couple and to the generation and education of children. According to the original divine plan this conjugal union is indissoluble, as Jesus Christ affirmed: "What therefore God has joined together, let no man put asunder" (Mark 10:9).

339. How does sin threaten marriage?

1606-1608   Because of original sin, which caused a rupture in the God-given communion between man and woman, the union of marriage is very often threatened by discord and infidelity. However, God in his infinite mercy gives to man and woman the grace to bring the union of their lives into accord with the original divine plan.

340. What does the Old Testament teach about marriage?

1609-1611   God helped his people above all through the teaching of the Law and the Prophets to deepen progressively their understanding of the unity and indissolubility of marriage. The nuptial covenant of God with Israel prepared for and prefigured the new covenant established by Jesus Christ the Son of God, with his spouse, the Church.

341. What new element did Christ give to Matrimony?

1612-1617   Christ not only restored the original order of matrimony but raised
1661   it to the dignity of a sacrament, giving spouses a special grace to live out their marriage as a symbol of Christ's love for his bride the Church: "Husbands, love your wives, as Christ loved the Church" (Ephesians 5:25).

342. Are all obliged to get married?

1618-1620   Matrimony is not an obligation for everyone, especially since God calls some men and women to follow the Lord Jesus in a life of virginity or of celibacy for the sake of the Kingdom of Heaven. These renounce the great good of Matrimony to concentrate on the things of the Lord and seek to please him. They become a sign of the absolute supremacy of Christ's love and of the ardent expectation of his glorious return.

343. How is the sacrament of Matrimony celebrated?

Since Matrimony establishes spouses in a public state of life in 1621-1624
the Church, its liturgical celebration is public, taking place in the
presence of a priest (or of a witness authorized by the Church) and
other witnesses.

344. What is matrimonial consent?

Matrimonial consent is given when a man and a woman manifest 1625-1632
the will to give themselves to each other irrevocably in order to live 1662-1663
a covenant of faithful and fruitful love. Since consent constitutes
Matrimony, it is indispensable and irreplaceable. For a valid marriage the consent must have as its object true Matrimony, and be a
human act which is conscious and free and not determined by duress
or coercion.

345. What is required when one of the spouses is not a Catholic?

A *mixed* marriage (between a Catholic and a baptized non-Catholic) 1633-1637
needs for liceity the permission of ecclesiastical authority. In a case of
disparity of cult (between a Catholic and a non-baptized person) a dis-
pensation is required for validity. In both cases, it is essential that the
spouses do not exclude the acceptance of the essential ends and prop-
erties of marriage. It is also necessary for the Catholic party to accept
the obligation, of which the non-Catholic party has been advised, to
persevere in the faith and to assure the baptism and Catholic education of their children.

346. What are the effects of the sacrament of Matrimony?

The sacrament of Matrimony establishes a perpetual and exclu- 1638-1642
sive *bond* between the spouses. God himself seals the consent of the
spouses. Therefore, a marriage which is ratified and consummated
between baptized persons can never be dissolved. Furthermore, this
sacrament bestows upon the spouses the grace necessary to attain
holiness in their married life and to accept responsibly the gift of children and provide for their education.

347. What sins are gravely opposed to the sacrament of Matrimony?

1645-1648   Adultery and polygamy are opposed to the sacrament of matrimony because they contradict the equal dignity of man and woman and the unity and exclusivity of married love. Other sins include the deliberate refusal of one's procreative potential which deprives conjugal love of the gift of children and divorce which goes against the indissolubility of marriage.

348. When does the Church allow the physical separation of spouses?

1629   The Church permits the physical separation of spouses when for seri-
1649   ous reasons their living together becomes practically impossible, even though there may be hope for their reconciliation. As long as one's spouse lives, however, one is not free to contract a new union, except if the marriage be null and be declared so by ecclesiastical authority.

349. What is the attitude of the Church toward those people who are divorced and then remarried?

1650-1651   The Church, since she is faithful to her Lord, cannot recognize the union of people who are civilly divorced and remarried. "Whoever divorces his wife and marries another, commits adultery against her; and if she divorces her husband and marries another, she commits adultery" (Mark 10:11-12). The Church manifests an attentive solicitude toward such people and encourages them to a life of faith, prayer, works of charity and the Christian education of their children. However, they cannot receive sacramental absolution, take Holy Communion, or exercise certain ecclesial responsibilities as long as their situation, which objectively contravenes God's law, persists.

350. Why is the Christian family called a *domestic church*?

1655-1658   The Christian family is called the domestic church because the fam-
1666   ily manifests and lives out the communal and familial nature of the Church as the family of God. Each family member, in accord with their own role, exercises the baptismal priesthood and contributes toward making the family a community of grace and of prayer, a school of human and Christian virtue and the place where the faith is first proclaimed to children.

CHAPTER FOUR
Other Liturgical Celebrations

THE SACRAMENTALS

351. What are the sacramentals?

These are sacred signs instituted by the Church to sanctify different   1667-1672
circumstances of life. They include a prayer accompanied by the sign   1677-1678
of the cross and other signs. Among the sacramentals which occupy
an important place are: blessings, which are the praise of God and a
prayer to obtain his gifts, the consecration of persons and the dedication of things for the worship of God.

352. What is an exorcism?

When the Church asks with its authority in the name of Jesus that a   1673
person or object be protected against the power of the Evil One and
withdrawn from his dominion, it is called an exorcism. This is done
in ordinary form in the rite of Baptism. A solemn exorcism, called
a *major exorcism,* can be performed only by a priest authorized by
the bishop.

353. What forms of popular piety accompany the sacramental life of the Church?

The religious sense of the Christian people has always found expres-   1674-1676
sion in the various forms of piety which accompany the sacramental   1679
life of the Church such as the veneration of relics, visits to sanctuar-
ies, pilgrimages, processions, the stations of the cross and the rosary.
The Church sheds the light of faith upon and fosters authentic forms
of popular piety.

CHRISTIAN FUNERALS

354. What is the relationship between the sacraments and the death of a Christian?

1680-1683   The Christian who dies in Christ reaches at the end of his earthly existence the fulfillment of that new life which was begun in Baptism, strengthened in Confirmation, and nourished in the Eucharist, the foretaste of the heavenly banquet. The meaning of the death of a Christian becomes clear in the light of the death and Resurrection of Christ our only hope. The Christian who dies in Christ Jesus goes "away from the body and at home with the Lord" (2 Corinthians 5:8).

355. What do funeral rites express?

1684-1685   Although celebrated in different rites in keeping with the situations and traditions of various regions, funerals express the paschal character of Christian death in hope of the resurrection. They also manifest the meaning of communion with the departed particularly through prayer for the purification of their souls.

356. What are the main moments in funerals?

1686-1690   Usually, funeral rites consist of four principal parts: welcoming the body of the deceased by the community with words of comfort and hope, the liturgy of the Word, the Eucharistic Sacrifice, and the farewell in which the soul of the departed is entrusted to God, the Source of eternal life, while the body is buried in the hope of the resurrection.

This illustration portrays the Last Supper with the institution of the Eucharist in a grand, carpeted hall off the ground floor (cf. Mark 14:15).

"While they were eating, Jesus took bread, said the blessing, broke it, and giving it to his disciples said, 'Take and eat; this is my body.' Then he took a cup, gave thanks, and gave it to them, saying, 'Drink from it, all of you, for this is my blood of the covenant, which will be shed on behalf of the many for the forgiveness of sins'" (Matthew 26:26-28).

In this image, Jesus is seated with the Apostles around a table in the form of a chalice. On the table are the Eucharistic species: bread and wine. The hall which is displayed against a very elaborate architectural backdrop with buildings and a circular tabernacle with seven columns symbolizes the Church which is the abode of the Eucharistic Christ. A significant detail is offered by the Apostle John who rests his head upon Jesus' chest (cf. John 13:25). He displays the communion of love which the Eucharist produces in the faithful. It is the response of the disciple to the invitation of the Master:

"I am the vine, you are the branches. Whoever remains in me and I in him will bear much fruit. . . . Remain in my love. If you keep my commandments, you will remain in my love" (John 15:5, 9-10).

The Eucharist is communion with Jesus and spiritual food to support the faithful in his daily struggle to keep the commandments:

"The Savior . . . is always and wholly present to those who live in him. He provides for their every need. He is everything for them and does not allow them to turn their glance to any other thing or to seek any thing apart from him. Indeed there is nothing the saints need but him: he gives them life and growth; he nourishes them; he is their light and breath; he molds in them the image of himself; he shines with the light of himself upon it and then offers himself to their sight. He is at once the nourishment and the One who nourishes. It is he who offers the bread of life and that which he offers is himself, the life of the living, fragrance to the one who breathes, the garment to the one who would put it on. Again it is he who enables us to walk and he is the way and also the place of rest, the end. We are his members; he is the head: is there need to do battle? He fights along with us and it is he who assigns victory to whom the honor is given. Do we win? Behold, he is the crown. Thus from every direction he leads our mind back to him and he does not allow us to turn to anything else nor be captivated by love of something else . . . From what we have said it should be clear that life in Christ does not concern the future only; rather it is already present for the saints who live and act in it" (N. Cabasilas, *Life in Christ*, 1, 13-15).

Jacob Copista, Illustration from the *Tetraevangelo*, Library of the Mechitarist Fathers, Vienna. (Used with permission.)

PART THREE
LIFE IN CHRIST

SECTION ONE
MAN'S VOCATION:
LIFE IN THE SPIRIT

Mary, the *Panhagia (all holy)*, is the masterpiece of the Holy Spirit (*Panhagion*). Her existence, from her immaculate conception to her glorious assumption into heaven, is completely sustained by the love of God. The Spirit of the Love of the Father and the Son makes of Mary a new creature, the new Eve. Her heart and mind are intent upon the adoration of and obedience to the heavenly Father. She is his beloved daughter and she is also dedicated to the acceptance and service of the Son whose mother and disciple she is. Her soul is likewise intent upon her surrender to and cooperation with the Holy Spirit for whom she is a treasured sanctuary.

In this image Mary is surrounded by angels playing musical instruments and making merry, her head crowned with the divine love of the Holy Spirit, symbolized by the dove. Mary is the mother and protector of the Church (at her feet there is a faint glimpse of a sacred edifice). Through her efficacious, motherly intercession with Jesus, she pours out upon the Church the abundance of heavenly graces (symbolized by the tuft of blooming roses).

Below at the left, the Apostle John in contemplation of Immaculate Mary represents every one of the faithful who sees in the Blessed Virgin the perfect model and likewise the teacher and guide for living in the Spirit.

The Cistercian abbot Christian (12th century) reflected upon how the Apostles shared with Mary their spiritual experiences. Comparing them to the twelve stars which crown the Blessed Virgin, he wrote:

"Frequently they gathered around the most prudent Virgin like disciples around their teacher to learn more fully the truth about what she had done, the truth that they would preach to others at the right moment. Since she was divinely set apart and taught, she showed herself to be a true storehouse of heavenly wisdom since in her daily life she had been close as a singular companion to wisdom itself, namely her Son, and had taken to heart and faithfully kept the things she had seen and heard" (*Sermon I on the Assumption of Blessed Mary*).

El Greco, *Saint John Contemplates the Immaculate Conception*, Church of Saint Leocadia and Saint Román; Museum of Santa Cruz, Toledo. (Used with permission.)

357. How is the Christian moral life bound up with faith and the sacraments?

What the symbol of faith professes, the sacraments communicate. Indeed, through them the faithful receive the grace of Christ and the gifts of the Holy Spirit which give them the capability of living a new life as children of God in Christ whom they have received in faith.

1691-1698

"O Christian, recognize your dignity." (Saint Leo the Great)

CHAPTER ONE
The Dignity of the Human Person

MAN THE IMAGE OF GOD

358. What is the root of human dignity?

The dignity of the human person is rooted in his or her creation in the image and likeness of God. Endowed with a spiritual and immortal soul, intelligence and free will, the human person is ordered to God and called in soul and in body to eternal beatitude.

1699-1715

OUR VOCATION TO BEATITUDE

359. How do we attain beatitude?

We attain beatitude by virtue of the grace of Christ which makes us participants in the divine life. Christ in the Gospel points out to his followers the way that leads to eternal happiness: the beatitudes. The grace of Christ also is operative in every person who, following a correct conscience, seeks and loves the true and the good and avoids evil.

1716

360. Why are the beatitudes important for us?

The beatitudes are at the heart of Jesus' preaching and they take up and fulfill the promises that God made starting with Abraham. They

1716-1717
1725-1726

depict the very countenance of Jesus and they characterize authentic Christian life. They reveal the ultimate goal of human activity, which is eternal happiness.

361. What is the relationship between the beatitudes and our desire for happiness?

1718-1719 The beatitudes respond to the innate desire for happiness that God has placed in the human heart in order to draw us to himself. God alone can satisfy this desire.

362. What is eternal happiness?

1720-1724
1727-1729 It is the vision of God in eternal life in which we are fully "partakers of the divine nature" (2 Peter 1:4), of the glory of Christ and of the joy of the trinitarian life. This happiness surpasses human capabilities. It is a supernatural and gratuitous gift of God just as is the grace which leads to it. This promised happiness confronts us with decisive moral choices concerning earthly goods and urges us to love God above all things.

MAN'S FREEDOM

363. What is freedom?

1730-1733
1743-1744 Freedom is the power given by God to act or not to act, to do this or to do that, and so to perform deliberate actions on one's own responsibility. Freedom characterizes properly human acts. The more one does what is good, the freer one becomes. Freedom attains its proper perfection when it is directed toward God, the highest good and our beatitude. Freedom implies also the possibility of choosing between good and evil. The choice of evil is an abuse of freedom and leads to the slavery of sin.

364. What is the relationship between freedom and responsibility?

1734-1737
1745-1746 Freedom makes people responsible for their actions to the extent that they are voluntary, even if the imputability and responsibility for an action can be diminished or sometimes cancelled by ignorance, inadvertence, duress, fear, inordinate attachments, or habit.

365. Why does everyone have a right to exercise freedom?

The right to the exercise of freedom belongs to everyone because it 1738
is inseparable from his or her dignity as a human person. Therefore 1747
this right must always be respected, especially in moral and religious
matters, and it must be recognized and protected by civil authority
within the limits of the common good and a just public order.

366. What place does human freedom have in the plan of salvation?

Our freedom is weakened because of original sin. This weakness is 1739-1742
intensified because of successive sins. Christ, however, set us free "so 1748
that we should remain free" (Galatians 5:1). With his grace, the Holy
Spirit leads us to spiritual freedom to make us free co-workers with
him in the Church and in the world.

367. What are the sources of the morality of human acts?

The morality of human acts depends on three sources: *the object cho-* 1749-1754
sen, either a true or apparent good; *the intention* of the subject who 1757-1758
acts, that is, the purpose for which the subject performs the act; and
the circumstances of the act, which include its consequences.

368. When is an act morally good?

An act is morally good when it assumes simultaneously the goodness 1755-1756
of the object, of the end, and of the circumstances. A chosen object 1759-1760
can by itself vitiate an act in its entirety, even if the intention is good.
It is not licit to do evil so that good may result from it. An evil end cor-
rupts the action, even if the object is good in itself. On the other hand,
a good end does not make an act good if the object of that act is evil,
since the end does not justify the means. Circumstances can increase
or diminish the responsibility of the one who is acting but they cannot change the moral quality of the acts themselves. They never make
good an act which is in itself evil.

369. Are there acts which are always illicit?

There are some acts which, in and of themselves, are always illicit by 1756, 1761
reason of their object (for example, blasphemy, homicide, adultery).
Choosing such acts entails a disorder of the will, that is, a moral evil

which can never be justified by appealing to the good effects which could possibly result from them.

The Morality of the Passions

370. What are the passions?

1762-1766
1771-1772
The passions are the feelings, the emotions or the movements of the sensible appetite—natural components of human psychology—which incline a person to act or not to act in view of what is perceived as good or evil. The principal passions are love and hatred, desire and fear, joy, sadness, and anger. The chief passion is love which is drawn by the attraction of the good. One can only love what is good, real or apparent.

371. Are the passions morally good or bad?

1767-1770
1773-1775
The passions insofar as they are movements of the sensible appetite are neither good nor bad in themselves. They are good when they contribute to a good action and they are evil in the opposite case. They can be taken up into the virtues or perverted by the vices.

The Moral Conscience

372. What is the moral conscience?

1776-1780
1795-1797
Moral conscience, present in the heart of the person, is a judgment of reason which at the appropriate moment enjoins him to do good and to avoid evil. Thanks to moral conscience, the human person perceives the moral quality of an act to be done or which has already been done, permitting him to assume responsibility for the act. When attentive to moral conscience, the prudent person can hear the voice of God who speaks to him or her.

373. What does the dignity of the human person imply for the moral conscience?

1780-1782
1798
The dignity of a human person requires the uprightness of a moral conscience (which is to say that it be in accord with what is just and good according to reason and the law of God). Because of this

personal dignity, no one may be forced to act contrary to conscience; nor, within the limits of the common good, be prevented from acting according to it, especially in religious matters.

374. How is a moral conscience formed to be upright and truthful?

An upright and true moral conscience is formed by education and by assimilating the Word of God and the teaching of the Church. It is supported by the gifts of the Holy Spirit and helped by the advice of wise people. Prayer and an examination of conscience can also greatly assist one's moral formation. 1783-1788
1799-1800

375. What norms must conscience always follow?

There are three general norms: (1) one may never do evil so that good may result from it; (2) the so-called *Golden Rule*, "Whatever you wish that men would do to you, do so to them" (Matthew 7:12); (3) charity always proceeds by way of respect for one's neighbor and his conscience, even though this does not mean accepting as good something that is objectively evil. 1789

376. Can a moral conscience make erroneous judgments?

A person must always obey the certain judgment of his own conscience but he could make erroneous judgments for reasons that may not always exempt him from personal guilt. However, an evil act committed through involuntary ignorance is not imputable to the person, even though the act remains objectively evil. One must therefore work to correct the errors of moral conscience. 1790-1794
1801-1802

THE VIRTUES

377. What is a virtue?

A virtue is a habitual and firm disposition to do the good. "The goal of a virtuous life is to become like God" (Saint Gregory of Nyssa). There are human virtues and theological virtues. 1803, 1833

378. What are the human virtues?

1804
1810-1811
1834, 1839

The human virtues are habitual and stable perfections of the intellect and will that govern our actions, order our passions and guide our conduct according to reason and faith. They are acquired and strengthened by the repetition of morally good acts and they are purified and elevated by divine grace.

379. What are the principal human virtues?

1805
1834

The principal human virtues are called the *cardinal* virtues, under which all the other virtues are grouped and which are the hinges of a virtuous life. The cardinal virtues are: prudence, justice, fortitude, and temperance.

380. What is prudence?

1806
1835

Prudence disposes reason to discern in every circumstance our true good and to choose the right means for achieving it. Prudence guides the other virtues by pointing out their rule and measure.

381. What is justice?

1807
1836

Justice consists in the firm and constant will to give to others their due. Justice toward God is called "the virtue of religion."

382. What is fortitude?

1808
1838

Fortitude assures firmness in difficulties and constancy in the pursuit of the good. It reaches even to the ability of possibly sacrificing one's own life for a just cause.

383. What is temperance?

1809
1838

Temperance moderates the attraction of pleasures, assures the mastery of the will over instincts and provides balance in the use of created goods.

384. What are the theological virtues?

1812-1813
1840-1841

The theological virtues have God himself as their origin, motive and direct object. Infused with sanctifying grace, they bestow on one the capacity to live in a relationship with the Trinity. They are the foundation and the energizing force of the Christian's moral activity and they give life to the human virtues. They are the pledge of the presence and action of the Holy Spirit in the faculties of the human being.

385. What are the theological virtues?

The theological virtues are faith, hope, and charity.

1813

386. What is the virtue of faith?

Faith is the theological virtue by which we believe in God and all that he has revealed to us and that the Church proposes for our belief because God is Truth itself. By faith the human person freely commits himself to God. Therefore, the believer seeks to know and do the will of God because "faith works through charity" (Galatians 5:6).

1814-1816
1842

387. What is hope?

Hope is the theological virtue by which we desire and await from God eternal life as our happiness, placing our trust in Christ's promises and relying on the help of the grace of the Holy Spirit to merit it and to persevere to the end of our earthly life.

1817-1821
1843

388. What is charity?

Charity is the theological virtue by which we love God above all things and our neighbor as ourselves for the love of God. Jesus makes charity the new commandment, the fullness of the law. It is the "bond of perfection" (Colossians 3:14) and the foundation of the other virtues to which it gives life, inspiration, and order. Without charity "I am nothing" and "I gain nothing" (1 Corinthians 13:2-3).

1822-1829
1844

389. What are the gifts of the Holy Spirit?

The gifts of the Holy Spirit are permanent dispositions which make us docile in following divine inspirations. They are seven: wisdom, understanding, counsel, fortitude, knowledge, piety, and fear of the Lord.

1830-1831
1845

390. What are the fruits of the Holy Spirit?

1832 The *fruits* of the Holy Spirit are perfections formed in us as the first fruits of eternal glory. The tradition of the Church lists twelve of them: charity, joy, peace, patience, kindness, goodness, generosity, gentleness, faithfulness, modesty, self-control, and chastity (Galatians 5:22-23, Vulgate).

Sɪɴ

391. What does the acceptance of God's mercy require from us?

1846-1848 It requires that we admit our faults and repent of our sins. God him-
1870 self by his Word and his Spirit lays bare our sins and gives us the truth of conscience and the hope of forgiveness.

392. What is sin?

1849-1851 Sin is "a word, an act, or a desire contrary to the eternal Law" (Saint
1871-1872 Augustine). It is an offense against God in disobedience to his love. It wounds human nature and injures human solidarity. Christ in his Passion fully revealed the seriousness of sin and overcame it with his mercy.

393. Is there a variety of sins?

1852-1853 There are a great many kinds of sins. They can be distinguished
1873 according to their object or according to the virtues or commandments which they violate. They can directly concern God, neighbor, or ourselves. They can also be divided into sins of thought, of word, of deed, or of omission.

394. How are sins distinguished according to their gravity?

1854 A distinction is made between mortal and venial sin.

395. When does one commit a mortal sin?

1855-1861 One commits a mortal sin when there are simultaneously pres-
1874 ent: grave matter, full knowledge, and deliberate consent. This sin destroys charity in us, deprives us of sanctifying grace, and, if unrepented, leads us to the eternal death of hell. It can be forgiven in the

ordinary way by means of the sacraments of Baptism and of Penance
or Reconciliation.

396. When does one commit a venial sin?

One commits a venial sin, which is essentially different from a mor-   1862-1864
tal sin, when the matter involved is less serious or, even if it is grave,   1875
when full knowledge or complete consent are absent. Venial sin does
not break the covenant with God but it weakens charity and manifests a disordered affection for created goods. It impedes the progress of a soul in the exercise of the virtues and in the practice of moral
good. It merits temporal punishment which purifies.

397. How does sin proliferate?

Sin creates a proclivity to sin; it engenders vice by repetition of the   1865, 1876
same acts.

398. What are vices?

Vices are the opposite of virtues. They are perverse habits which   1866-1867
darken the conscience and incline one to evil. The vices can be linked
to the seven so-called *capital* sins which are: pride, avarice, envy,
anger, lust, gluttony, and sloth or acedia.

399. Do we have any responsibility for sins committed by others?

We do have such a responsibility when we culpably cooperate   1868
with them.

400. What are *structures* of sin?

Structures of sin are social situations or institutions that are contrary   1869
to the divine law. They are the expression and effect of personal sins.

CHAPTER TWO
The Human Community

THE PERSON AND SOCIETY

401. In what does the social dimension of man consist?

1877-1880   Together with the personal call to beatitude, the human person has
1890-1891   a communal dimension as an essential component of his nature and
vocation. Indeed, all are called to the same end, God himself. There is
a certain resemblance between the communion of the divine Persons
and the fraternity that people are to establish among themselves in
truth and love. Love of neighbor is inseparable from love for God.

402. What is the relationship between the person and society?

1881-1882   The human *person* is and ought to be the principle, the subject and
1892-1893   the end of all social institutions. Certain societies, such as the family
and the civic community, are necessary for the human person. Also
helpful are other associations on the national and international levels
with due respect for the principle of *subsidiarity*.

403. What is the principle of subsidiarity?

1883-1885   The principle of subsidiarity states that a community of a higher
1894   order should not assume the task belonging to a community of a
lower order and deprive it of its authority. It should rather support it
in case of need.

404. What else is required for an authentic human society?

1886-1889   Authentic human society requires respect for justice, a just hierar-
1895-1896   chy of values, and the subordination of material and instinctual
dimensions to interior and spiritual ones. In particular, where sin
has perverted the social climate, it is necessary to call for the conversion of hearts and for the grace of God to obtain social changes that
may really serve each person and the whole person. Charity, which
requires and makes possible the practice of justice, is the greatest
social commandment.

PARTICIPATION IN SOCIAL LIFE

405. What is the foundation of the authority of society?

Every human community needs a legitimate authority that preserves order and contributes to the realization of the common good. The foundation of such authority lies in human nature because it corresponds to the order established by God. 1897-1902 1918-1920

406. When is authority exercised in a legitimate way?

Authority is exercised legitimately when it acts for the common good and employs morally licit means to attain it. Therefore, political regimes must be determined by the free decision of their citizens. They should respect the principle of the "rule of law" in which the law, and not the arbitrary will of some, is sovereign. Unjust laws and measures contrary to the moral order are not binding in conscience. 1901-1904 1921-1922

407. What is the common good?

By the common good is meant the sum total of those conditions of social life which allow people as groups and as individuals to reach their proper fulfillment. 1905-1906 1924

408. What is involved in the common good?

The common good involves: respect for and promotion of the fundamental rights of the person, the development of the spiritual and temporal goods of persons and society, and the peace and security of all. 1907-1909 1925

409. Where can one find the most complete realization of the common good?

The most complete realization of the common good is found in those political communities which defend and promote the good of their citizens and of intermediate groups without forgetting the universal good of the entire human family. 1910-1912 1927

410. How does one participate in bringing about the common good?

1913-1917
1926

All men and women according to the place and role that they occupy participate in promoting the common good by respecting just laws and taking charge of the areas for which they have personal responsibility such as the care of their own family and the commitment to their own work. Citizens also should take an active part in public life as far as possible.

SOCIAL JUSTICE

411. How does society ensure social justice?

1928-1933
1943-1944

Society ensures social justice when it respects the dignity and the rights of the person as the proper end of society itself. Furthermore, society pursues social justice, which is linked to the common good and to the exercise of authority, when it provides the conditions that allow associations and individuals to obtain what is their due.

412. On what is human equality based?

1934-1935
1945

All persons enjoy equal dignity and fundamental rights insofar as they are created in the image of the one God, are endowed with the same rational soul, have the same nature and origin, and are called in Christ, the one and only Savior, to the same divine beatitude.

413. How are we to view social inequalities?

1936-1938
1946-1947

There are sinful social and economic inequalities which affect millions of human beings. These inequalities are in open contradiction to the Gospel and are contrary to justice, to the dignity of persons, and to peace. There are, however, differences among people caused by various factors which enter into the plan of God. Indeed, God wills that each might receive what he or she needs from others and that those endowed with particular talents should share them with others. Such differences encourage and often oblige people to the practice of generosity, kindness and the sharing of goods. They also foster the mutual enrichment of cultures.

414. How is human solidarity manifested?

Solidarity, which springs from human and Christian brotherhood, is manifested in the first place by the just distribution of goods, by a fair remuneration for work and by zeal for a more just social order. The *virtue* of solidarity also practices the sharing of the spiritual goods of faith which is even more important than sharing material goods.

1939-1942
1948

CHAPTER THREE
God's Salvation: Law and Grace

THE MORAL LAW

415. What is the moral law?

The moral law is a work of divine Wisdom. It prescribes the ways and the rules of conduct that lead to the promised beatitude and it forbids the ways that turn away from God.

1950-1953
1975-1978

416. In what does the natural moral law consist?

The natural law which is inscribed by the Creator on the heart of every person consists in a participation in the wisdom and the goodness of God. It expresses that original moral sense which enables one to discern by reason the good and the bad. It is universal and immutable and determines the basis of the duties and fundamental rights of the person as well as those of the human community and civil law.

1954-1960
1978-1979

417. Is such a law perceived by everyone?

Because of sin the natural law is not always perceived nor is it recognized by everyone with equal clarity and immediacy.

1960

> For this reason God "wrote on the tables of the Law what men did not read in their hearts." (Saint Augustine)

418. What is the relationship between the natural law and the Old Law?

1961-1962
1980

The Old Law is the first stage of revealed Law. It expresses many truths naturally accessible to reason and which are thus affirmed and authenticated in the covenant of salvation. Its moral prescriptions, which are summed up in the Ten Commandments of the Decalogue, lay the foundations of the human vocation, prohibit what is contrary to the love of God and neighbor, and prescribe what is essential to it.

419. What place does the Old Law have in the plan of salvation?

1963-1964
1982

The Old Law permitted one to know many truths which are accessible to reason, showed what must or must not be done and, above all, like a wise tutor, prepared and disposed one for conversion and for the acceptance of the Gospel. However, while being holy, spiritual, and good, the Old Law was still imperfect because in itself it did not give the strength and the grace of the Spirit for its observance.

420. What is the New Law or the Law of the Gospel?

1965-1972
1983-1985

The New Law or the Law of the Gospel, proclaimed and fulfilled by Christ, is the fullness and completion of the divine law, natural and revealed. It is summed up in the commandment to love God and neighbor and to love one another as Christ loved us. It is also an interior reality: the grace of the Holy Spirit which makes possible such love. It is the "law of freedom" (James 1:25) because it inclines us to act spontaneously by the prompting of charity.

> *"The New Law is mainly the same grace of the Holy Spirit which is given to believers in Christ."* (Saint Thomas Aquinas)

421. Where does one find the New Law?

1971-1974
1986

The New Law is found in the entire life and preaching of Christ and in the moral catechesis of the Apostles. The Sermon on the Mount is its principal expression.

GRACE AND JUSTIFICATION

422. What is justification?

Justification is the most excellent work of God's love. It is the merciful and freely-given act of God which takes away our sins and makes us just and holy in our whole being. It is brought about by means of the grace of the Holy Spirit which has been merited for us by the Passion of Christ and is given to us in Baptism. Justification is the beginning of the free response of man, that is, faith in Christ and of cooperation with the grace of the Holy Spirit.

1987-1995
2017-2020

423. What is the grace that justifies?

That grace is the gratuitous gift that God gives us to make us participants in his trinitarian life and able to act by his love. It is called *habitual, sanctifying or deifying grace* because it sanctifies and divinizes us. It is *supernatural* because it depends entirely on God's gratuitous initiative and surpasses the abilities of the intellect and the powers of human beings. It therefore escapes our experience.

1996-1998
2005
2021

424. What other kinds of grace are there?

Besides habitual grace, there are actual graces (gifts for specific circumstances), sacramental graces (gifts proper to each sacrament), special graces or charisms (gifts that are intended for the common good of the Church), among which are the graces of state that accompany the exercise of ecclesial ministries and the responsibilities of life.

1999-2000
2003-2004
2023-2024

425. What is the relationship between grace and human freedom?

Grace precedes, prepares and elicits our free response. It responds to the deep yearnings of human freedom, calls for its cooperation and leads freedom toward its perfection.

2001-2002

426. What is merit?

In general merit refers to the right to recompense for a good deed. With regard to God, we of ourselves are not able to merit anything, having received everything freely from him. However, God gives us the possibility of acquiring merit through union with the love of Christ, who is the source of our merits before God. The merits for

2006-2010
2025-2027

good works, therefore must be attributed in the first place to the grace of God and then to the free will of man.

427. What are the goods that we can merit?

2010-2011
2027

Moved by the Holy Spirit, we can merit for ourselves and for others the graces needed for our sanctification and for the attainment of eternal life. Even temporal goods, suitable for us, can be merited in accordance with the plan of God. No one, however, can merit the *initial grace* which is at the origin of conversion and justification.

428. Are all called to Christian holiness?

2012-2016
2028-2029

All the faithful are called to Christian holiness. This is the fullness of Christian life and the perfection of charity and it is brought about by intimate union with Christ and, in him, with the most Holy Trinity. The path to holiness for a Christian goes by way of the cross and will come to its fulfillment in the final resurrection of the just, in which God will be all in all.

THE CHURCH, MOTHER AND TEACHER

429. How does the Church nourish the moral life of a Christian?

2030-2031
2047

The Church is the community in which the Christian receives the Word of God, the teachings of the "law of Christ" (Galatians 6:2), and the grace of the sacraments. Christians are united to the Eucharistic sacrifice of Christ in such a way that their moral life is an act of spiritual worship; and they learn the example of holiness from the Virgin Mary and the lives of the Saints.

430. Why does the Magisterium of the Church act in the field of morality?

2032-2040
2049-2051

It is the duty of the Magisterium of the Church to preach the faith that is to be believed and put into practice in life. This duty extends even to the specific precepts of the natural law because their observance is necessary for salvation.

431. What purpose do the precepts of the Church have?

The five precepts of the Church are meant to guarantee for the faith- 2041
ful the indispensable minimum in the spirit of prayer, the sacramen- 2048
tal life, moral commitment and growth in love of God and neighbor.

432. What are the precepts of the Church?

They are: (1) to attend Mass on Sundays and other holy days of obliga- 2042-2043
tion and to refrain from work and activities which could impede the
sanctification of those days; (2) to confess one's sins, receiving the sacrament of Reconciliation at least once each year; (3) to receive the sacrament of the Eucharist at least during the Easter season; (4) to abstain
from eating meat and to observe the days of fasting established by
the Church; and (5) to help to provide for the material needs of the
Church, each according to his own ability.

433. Why is the Christian moral life indispensable for the proclamation of the Gospel?

Because their lives are conformed to the Lord Jesus, Christians draw 2044-2046
others to faith in the true God, build up the Church, inform the world
with the spirit of the Gospel, and hasten the coming of the Kingdom
of God.

SECTION TWO
THE TEN COMMANDMENTS

A young man addressed this question to Jesus: "Teacher, what good must I do to gain eternal life?" (Matthew 19:16). Jesus answered him: "If you wish to enter into life, keep the commandments" and he immediately added: "come, follow me" (Matthew 19:17, 21)

Following Jesus implies observing the commandments. The Old Law has not been abolished; man is rather invited to find it in the person of the divine Master who realized it perfectly in himself, revealed its full meaning, and attested to its perennial value.

The image in this section presents Christ who teaches his disciples in the so-called *Sermon on the Mount* (cf. Matthew 5-7). The principal parts of this "sermon" are: the beatitudes, the fulfillment of the old law, the prayer, the *Our Father*, instructions on fasting, and the invitation to the disciples to be the salt of the earth and the light of the world.

The mountain with its elevation above the earth and its closeness to heaven describes a privileged place of encounter with God. Jesus the teacher, seated on the rock as on a favored chair with the index finger of his right hand pointed to heaven, indicates the divine origin of his words of life and happiness. The scroll which he holds in his left hand signifies the fulfillment of his teaching which he entrusts with confidence to the Apostles who are invited to preach the Gospel to all nations, baptizing them in the name of the Father, Son, and Holy Spirit.

The twelve Apostles who are the crown at the feet of the Master all have a halo to show their loyalty to Christ and the testimony of their holiness in the Church. Only one of them, half hidden at the right, has a black halo, suggesting his infidelity to the good news. The proclamation of the kingdom of God by Jesus was not an empty and inconsistent word but an efficacious and effective action. The story of the paralytic at Capernaum, related by the three synoptics, is significant in this respect:

"He entered a boat, made the crossing, and came into his own town. And there people brought to him a paralytic lying on a stretcher. When Jesus saw their faith, he said to the paralytic, 'Courage, child, your sins are forgiven.' At that, some of the scribes said to themselves, 'This man is blaspheming.' Jesus knew what they were thinking, and said, 'Why, do you harbor evil thoughts? Which is easier, to say "Your sins are forgiven," or to say "Rise and walk"? But that you may know that the Son of Man has authority on earth to forgive sins'—he then said to the paralytic, 'Rise, pick up your stretcher, and go home.' He rose and went home" (Matthew 9:1-7).

In this episode, the physical cure is nothing other than the visible face of the spiritual miracle of the liberation from sin. Healing and forgiving are typical gestures of the teaching activity of Jesus, the divine Master.

Beato Angelico, *The Sermon on the Mount*, Museum of Saint Mark, Florence. (Photo credit: Scala/Art Resource, NY.)

EXODUS 20:2-17	DEUTERONOMY 5:6-7, 11-12, 16-21	A TRADITIONAL CATECHETICAL FORMULA
I am the LORD your God, who brought you out of the land of Egypt, out of the house of bondage. You shall have no other gods before me. You shall not make for yourself a graven image, or any likeness of anything that is in heaven above, or that is in the earth beneath, or that is in the water under the earth; you shall not bow down to them or serve them; for I the LORD your God am a jealous God, visiting the iniquity of the fathers upon the children to the third and the fourth generation of those who hate me, but showing steadfast love to thousands of those who love me and keep my commandments.	I am the LORD your God, who brought you out of the land of Egypt, out of the house of bondage. You shall have no other gods before me. . . .	1. I am the LORD your God: you shall not have strange gods before me.
You shall not take the name of the LORD your God in vain; for the LORD will not hold him guiltless who takes his name in vain.	You shall not take the name of the LORD your God in vain. . . .	2. You shall not take the name of the LORD your God in vain.

EXODUS 20:2-17	DEUTERONOMY 5:6-7, 11-12, 16-21	A TRADITIONAL CATECHETICAL FORMULA
Remember the sabbath day, to keep it holy. Six days you shall labor, and do all your work; but the seventh day is a sabbath to the LORD your God; in it you shall not do any work, you, or your son, or your daughter, your manservant, or your maidservant, or your cattle, or the sojourner who is within your gates; for in six days the LORD made heaven and earth, the sea, and all that is in them, and rested the seventh day; therefore the LORD blessed the sabbath day and hallowed it.	Observe the sabbath day, to keep it holy. . . .	3. Remember to keep holy the LORD's day.
Honor your father and your mother, that your days may be long in the land which the LORD your God gives you.	Honor your father and your mother. . . .	4. Honor your father and your mother.
You shall not kill.	You shall not kill.	5. You shall not kill.
You shall not commit adultery.	Neither shall you commit adultery.	6. You shall not commit adultery.
You shall not steal.	Neither shall you steal.	7. You shall not steal.

EXODUS 20:2-17	DEUTERONOMY 5:6-7, 11-12, 16-21	A TRADITIONAL CATECHETICAL FORMULA
You shall not bear false witness against your neighbor. You shall not covet your neighbor's house; you shall not covet your neighbor's wife, or his manservant, or his maidservant, or his ox, or his ass, or anything that is your neighbor's.	Neither shall you bear false witness against your neighbor. Neither shall you covet your neighbor's wife. . . . You shall not desire . . . anything that is your neighbor's.	8. You shall not bear false witness against your neighbor. 9. You shall not covet your neighbor's wife. 10. You shall not covet your neighbor's goods.

434. "Teacher, what good must I do to gain eternal life?" (Matthew 19:16).

To the young man who asked this question, Jesus answered, "If you wish to enter into life, keep the commandments," and then he added, "Come, follow me" (Matthew 19:17, 21). To follow Jesus involves keeping the commandments. The law has not been abolished but man is invited to rediscover it in the Person of the divine Master who realized it perfectly in himself, revealed its full meaning and attested to its permanent validity.

2052-2054
2075-2076

435. How did Jesus interpret the Law?

Jesus interpreted the Law in the light of the twofold yet single commandment of love, the fullness of the Law: "'You shall love the Lord your God with all your heart, and with all your soul, and with all your mind.' This is the greatest and first commandment. And the second is like it: You shall love your neighbor as yourself. On these two commandments depend all the law and the prophets" (Matthew 22:37-40).

2055

436. What does "Decalogue" mean?

Decalogue means "ten words" (Exodus 34:28). These words sum up the Law given by God to the people of Israel in the context of the

2056-2057

Covenant mediated by Moses. This Decalogue, in presenting the commandments of the love of God (the first three) and of one's neighbor (the other seven), traces for the chosen people and for every person in particular the path to a life freed from the slavery of sin.

437. What is the bond between the Decalogue and the Covenant?

2058-2063   The Decalogue must be understood in the light of the Covenant in
    2077   which God revealed himself and made known his will. In observing the commandments, the people manifested their belonging to God and they answered his initiative of love with thanksgiving.

438. What importance does the Church give to the Decalogue?

2064-2068   The Church, in fidelity to Scripture and to the example of Christ, acknowledges the primordial importance and significance of the Decalogue. Christians are obliged to keep it.

439. Why does the Decalogue constitute an organic unity?

2069   The Ten Commandments form an organic and indivisible whole
2079   because each commandment refers to the other commandments and to the entire Decalogue. To break one commandment, therefore, is to violate the entire law.

440. Why does the Decalogue enjoin serious obligations?

2072-2073   It does so because the Decalogue expresses the fundamental duties of
    2081   man towards God and towards his neighbor.

441. Is it possible to keep the Decalogue?

2074   Yes, because Christ without whom we can do nothing enables us to
2082   keep it with the gift of his Spirit and his grace.

CHAPTER ONE

"You Shall Love the Lord Your God with All Your Heart, with All Your Soul, and with All Your Mind"

THE FIRST COMMANDMENT: I AM THE LORD YOUR GOD, YOU SHALL NOT HAVE OTHER GODS BEFORE ME

442. What is implied in the affirmation of God: "I am the LORD your God" (Exodus 20:2)?

This means that the faithful must guard and activate the three theo-   2083-2094
logical virtues and must avoid sins which are opposed to them. *Faith*   2133-2134
believes in God and rejects everything that is opposed to it, such as,
deliberate doubt, unbelief, heresy, apostasy, and schism. *Hope* trust-
ingly awaits the blessed vision of God and his help, while avoiding
despair and presumption. *Charity* loves God above all things and
therefore repudiates indifference, ingratitude, lukewarmness, sloth
or spiritual indolence, and that hatred of God which is born of pride.

443. What is the meaning of the words of our Lord, "Adore the Lord your God and worship Him alone" (Matthew 4:10)?

These words mean to adore God as the Lord of everything that exists;   2095-2105
to render to him the individual and community worship which is   2135-2136
his due; to pray to him with sentiments of praise, of thanks, and of
supplication; to offer him sacrifices, above all the spiritual sacrifice of
one's own life, united with the perfect sacrifice of Christ; and to keep
the promises and vows made to him.

444. In what way does a person exercise his or her proper right to worship God in truth and in freedom?

Every person has the right and the moral duty to seek the truth,   2104-2109
especially in what concerns God and his Church. Once the truth is   2137
known, each person has the right and moral duty to embrace it, to
guard it faithfully and to render God authentic worship. At the same
time, the dignity of the human person requires that in religious matters no one may be forced to act against conscience nor be restrained,
within the just limits of public order, from acting in conformity with
conscience, privately or publicly, alone or in association with others.

445. What does God prohibit by his command, "You shall not have other gods before me" (Exodus 20:2)?

2110-2128   This commandment forbids:

2138-2140   *Polytheism* and *idolatry*, which divinizes creatures, power, money, or even demons.

Superstition which is a departure from the worship due to the true God and which also expresses itself in various forms of divination, magic, sorcery and spiritism.

Irreligion which is evidenced: in tempting God by word or deed; in sacrilege, which profanes sacred persons or sacred things, above all the Eucharist; and in simony, which involves the buying or selling of spiritual things.

Atheism which rejects the existence of God, founded often on a false conception of human autonomy.

Agnosticism which affirms that nothing can be known about God, and involves indifferentism and practical atheism.

446. Does the commandment of God, "You shall not make for yourself a graven image" (Exodus 20:4), forbid the cult of images?

2129-2132   In the Old Testament this commandment forbade any representation
2141   of God who is absolutely transcendent. The Christian veneration of sacred images, however, is justified by the incarnation of the Son of God (as taught by the Second Council of Nicea in A.D. 787) because such veneration is founded on the mystery of the Son of God made man, in whom the transcendent God is made visible. This does not mean the adoration of an image, but rather the veneration of the one who is represented in it: for example, Christ, the Blessed Virgin Mary, the Angels and the Saints.

THE SECOND COMMANDMENT: YOU SHALL NOT TAKE THE NAME OF THE LORD YOUR GOD IN VAIN

447. How does one respect the holiness of the Name of God?

2142-2149   One shows respect for the holy Name of God by blessing it, praising
2160-2162   it and glorifying it. It is forbidden, therefore, to call on the Name of God to justify a crime. It is also wrong to use the holy Name of God in any improper way as in *blasphemy* (which by its nature is a grave sin), *curses*, and *unfaithfulness* to promises made in the Name of God.

448. Why is a false oath forbidden?

It is forbidden because one calls upon God who is truth itself to be the   2150-2151
witness to a lie.   2163-2164

> *"Do not swear, whether by the Creator or by any creature, except*
> *truthfully, of necessity and with reverence."* (Saint Ignatius
> of Loyola)

449. What is perjury?

Perjury is to make a promise under oath with the intention of not   2152-2155
keeping it or to violate a promise made under oath. It is a grave sin
against God who is always faithful to his promises.

THE THIRD COMMANDMENT: REMEMBER TO KEEP HOLY THE LORD'S
DAY

450. Why did God "bless the Sabbath day and declare it sacred" (Exodus 20:11)?

God did so because on the Sabbath day one remembers *God's rest* on   2168-2172
the seventh day of creation, and also the liberation of Israel from slav-   2189
ery in Egypt and the Covenant which God sealed with his people.

451. How did Jesus act in regard to the Sabbath?

Jesus recognized the holiness of the Sabbath day and with divine   2173
authority he gave this law its authentic interpretation: "The sabbath
was made for man, not man for the sabbath" (Mark 2:27).

452. For what reason has the Sabbath been changed to Sunday for Christians?

The reason is because Sunday is the day of the Resurrection of Christ.   2174-2176
As "the first day of the week" (Mark 16:2) it recalls the first creation;   2190-2191
and as the "eighth day," which follows the sabbath, it symbolizes the
new creation ushered in by the Resurrection of Christ. Thus, it has
become for Christians the first of all days and of all feasts. It is the *day*

of the Lord in which he with his Passover fulfilled the spiritual truth of the Jewish Sabbath and proclaimed man's eternal rest in God.

453. How does one keep Sunday holy?

2177-2185   Christians keep Sunday and other days of obligation holy by partici-
2192-2193   pating in the Eucharist of the Lord and by refraining from those activities which impede the worship of God and disturb the joy proper to the day of the Lord or the necessary relaxation of mind and body. Activities are allowed on the Sabbath which are bound up with family needs or with important social service, provided that they do not lead to habits prejudicial to the holiness of Sunday, to family life and to health.

454. Why is the civil recognition of Sunday as a feast day important?

2186-2188   It is important so that all might be given the real possibility of enjoy-
2194-2195   ing sufficient rest and leisure to take care of their religious, familial, cultural and social lives. It is important also to have an opportune time for meditation, for reflection, for silence, for study, and a time to dedicate to good works, particularly for the sick and for the elderly.

CHAPTER TWO
"You Shall Love Your Neighbor as Yourself"

THE FOURTH COMMANDMENT: HONOR YOUR FATHER AND YOUR MOTHER

455. What does the fourth commandment require?

2196-2200   It commands us to honor and respect our parents and those whom
2247-2248   God, for our good, has vested with his authority.

456. What is the nature of the family in the plan of God?

2201-2205   A man and a woman united in marriage form a family together with
2249   their children. God instituted the family and endowed it with its

fundamental constitution. Marriage and the family are ordered to the good of the spouses and to the procreation and education of children. Members of the same family establish among themselves personal relationships and primary responsibilities. In Christ the family becomes the *domestic church* because it is a community of faith, of hope, and of charity.

457. What place does the family occupy in society?

The family is the original cell of human society and is, therefore, prior to any recognition by public authority. Family values and principles constitute the foundation of social life. Family life is an initiation into the life of society.

2207-2208

458. What are the duties that society has toward the family?

Society, while respecting the principle of subsidiarity, has the duty to support and strengthen marriage and the family. Public authority must respect, protect and foster the true nature of marriage and the family, public morality, the rights of parents, and domestic prosperity.

2209-2213
2250

459. What are the duties of children toward their parents?

Children owe respect (filial piety), gratitude, docility and obedience to their parents. In paying them respect and in fostering good relationships with their brothers and sisters, children contribute to the growth in harmony and holiness in family life in general. Adult children should give their parents material and moral support whenever they find themselves in situations of distress, sickness, loneliness, or old age.

2214-2220
2251

460. What are the duties of parents toward their children?

Parents, in virtue of their participation in the fatherhood of God, have the first responsibility for the education of their children and they are the first heralds of the faith for them. They have the duty to love and respect their children as *persons* and as *children of God* and to provide, as far as is possible, for their physical and spiritual needs. They should select for them a suitable school and help them with prudent counsel in the choice of their profession and their state of life. In

2221-2231

particular they have the mission of educating their children in the Christian faith.

461. How are parents to educate their children in the Christian faith?

2252-2253 Parents do this mainly by example, prayer, family catechesis and participation in the life of the Church.

462. Are family bonds an absolute good?

2232-2233 Family ties are important but not absolute, because the first vocation of a Christian is to follow Jesus and love him: "He who loves father or mother more than me is not worthy of me; and he who loves son or daughter more than me is not worthy of me" (Matthew 10:37). Parents must support with joy their children's choice to follow Jesus in whatever state of life, even in the consecrated life or the priestly ministry.

463. How should authority be exercised in the various spheres of civil society?

2234-2237 Authority should always be exercised as a service, respecting funda-
2254 mental human rights, a just hierarchy of values, laws, distributive justice, and the principle of subsidiarity. All those who exercise authority should seek the interests of the community before their own interest and allow their decisions to be inspired by the truth about God, about man and about the world.

464. What are the duties of citizens in regard to civil authorities?

2238-2241 Those subject to authority should regard those in authority as rep-
2255 resentatives of God and offer their loyal collaboration for the right functioning of public and social life. This collaboration includes love and service of one's homeland, the right and duty to vote, payment of taxes, the defense of one's country, and the right to exercise constructive criticism.

465. When is a citizen forbidden to obey civil authorities?

2242-2243 A citizen is obliged in conscience not to obey the laws of civil authori-
2256 ties when they are contrary to the demands of the moral order: "We must obey God rather than men" (Acts of the Apostles 5:29).

The Fifth Commandment: You Shall Not Kill

466. Why must human life be respected?

Human life must be respected because it is *sacred*. From its beginning   2258-2262
human life involves the creative action of God and it remains forever   2318-2320
in a special relationship with the Creator, who is its sole end. It is not
lawful for anyone directly to destroy an innocent human being. This
is gravely contrary to the dignity of the person and the holiness of the
Creator. "Do not slay the innocent and righteous" (Exodus 23:7).

467. Why is the legitimate defense of persons and of society not opposed to this norm?

Because in choosing to legitimately defend oneself one is respecting   2263-2265
the right to life (either one's own right to life or that of another) and
not choosing to kill. Indeed, for someone responsible for the life of
another, legitimate defense can be not only a right but a grave duty,
provided only that disproportionate force is not used.

468. What is the purpose of punishment?

A punishment imposed by legitimate public authority has the aim of   2266
redressing the disorder introduced by the offense, of defending public order and people's safety, and contributing to the correction of the
guilty party.

469. What kind of punishment may be imposed?

The punishment imposed must be proportionate to the gravity of the   2267
offense. Given the possibilities which the State now has for effectively
preventing crime by rendering one who has committed an offense
incapable of doing harm, the cases in which the execution of the
offender is an absolute necessity "are very rare, if not practically non-
existent" (*Evangelium Vitae*). When non-lethal means are sufficient,
authority should limit itself to such means because they better correspond to the concrete conditions of the common good, are more in
conformity with the dignity of the human person, and do not remove
definitively from the guilty party the possibility of reforming himself.

470. What is forbidden by the fifth commandment?

2268-2283
2321-2326

The fifth commandment forbids as gravely contrary to the moral law:

—direct and intentional murder and cooperation in it;

—direct abortion, willed as an end or as means, as well as cooperation in it. Attached to this sin is the penalty of excommunication because, from the moment of his or her conception, the human being must be absolutely respected and protected in his integrity;

—direct euthanasia which consists in putting an end to the life of the handicapped, the sick, or those near death by an act or by the omission of a required action;

—suicide and voluntary cooperation in it, insofar as it is a grave offense against the just love of God, of self, and of neighbor. One's responsibility may be aggravated by the scandal given; one who is psychologically disturbed or is experiencing grave fear may have diminished responsibility.

471. What medical procedures are permitted when death is considered imminent?

2278-2279

When death is considered imminent the ordinary care owed to a sick person cannot be legitimately interrupted. However, it is legitimate to use painkillers which do not aim at death and to refuse "over-zealous treatment," that is the utilization of disproportionate medical procedures without reasonable hope of a positive outcome.

472. Why must society protect every embryo?

2273-2274

The inalienable right to life of every human individual from the first moment of conception is a constitutive element of civil society and its legislation. When the State does not place its power at the service of the rights of all and in particular of the more vulnerable, including unborn children, the very foundations of a State based on law are undermined.

473. How does one avoid scandal?

2284-2287

Scandal, which consists in inducing others to do evil, is avoided when we respect the soul and body of the person. Anyone who deliberately leads others to commit serious sins himself commits a grave offense.

474. What duty do we have toward our body?

We must take reasonable *care of our own physical health* and that of   2288-2291
others but avoid the *cult of the body* and every kind of excess. Also to
be avoided are the use of drugs which cause very serious damage to
human health and life, as well as the abuse of food, alcohol, tobacco
and medicine.

475. When are scientific, medical, or psychological experiments on human individuals or groups morally legitimate?

They are morally legitimate when they are at the service of the inte-   2292-2295
gral good of the person and of society, without disproportionate risks
to the life and physical and psychological integrity of the subjects
who must be properly informed and consenting.

476. Are the transplant and donation of organs allowed before and after death?

The transplant of organs is morally acceptable with the consent of   2296
the donor and without excessive risks to him or her. Before allowing
the noble act of organ donation after death, one must verify that the
donor is truly dead.

477. What practices are contrary to respect for the bodily integrity of the human person?

They are: kidnapping and hostage taking, terrorism, torture, violence,   2297-2298
and direct sterilization. Amputations and mutilations of a person are
morally permissible only for strictly therapeutic medical reasons.

478. What care must be given to the dying?

The dying have a right to live the last moments of their earthly lives   2299
with dignity and, above all, to be sustained with prayer and the sacraments that prepare them to meet the living God.

479. How are the bodies of the deceased to be treated?

The bodies of the departed must be treated with love and respect.   2300-2301
Their cremation is permitted provided that it does not demonstrate a
denial of faith in the resurrection of the body.

480. What does the Lord ask of every person in regard to peace?

2302-2303 The Lord proclaimed *"Blessed* are the peacemakers" (Matthew 5:9; emphasis added). He called for peace of heart and denounced the immorality of anger which is a desire for revenge for some evil suffered. He also denounced hatred which leads one to wish evil on one's neighbor. These attitudes, if voluntary and consented to in matters of great importance, are mortal sins against charity.

481. What is peace in this world?

2304-2305 Peace in this world, which is required for the respect and development of human life, is not simply the absence of war or a balance of power between adversaries. It is "the tranquility of order" (Saint Augustine), "the work of justice" (Isaiah 32:17) and the effect of charity. Earthly peace is the image and fruit of the peace of Christ.

482. What is required for earthly peace?

2304
2307-2308 Earthly peace requires the equal distribution and safeguarding of the goods of persons, free communication among human beings, respect for the dignity of persons and peoples, and the assiduous practice of justice and fraternity.

483. When is it morally permitted to use military force?

2307-2310 The use of military force is morally justified when the following conditions are simultaneously present:
    —the suffering inflicted by the aggressor must be lasting, grave and certain;
    —all other peaceful means must have been shown to be ineffective;
    —there are well founded prospects of success;
    —the use of arms, especially given the power of modern weapons of mass destruction, must not produce evils graver than the evil to be eliminated.

484. In danger of war, who has the responsibility for the rigorous evaluation of these conditions?

2309 This responsibility belongs to the prudential judgment of government officials who also have the right to impose on citizens the obligation of national defense. The personal right to conscientious objection makes an exception to this obligation which should then be carried out by another form of service to the human community.

485. In case of war, what does the moral law require?

Even during a war the moral law always remains valid. It requires the humane treatment of noncombatants, wounded soldiers and prisoners of war. Deliberate actions contrary to the law of nations, and the orders that command such actions are crimes, which blind obedience does not excuse. Acts of mass destruction must be condemned and likewise the extermination of peoples or ethnic minorities, which are most grievous sins. One is morally bound to resist the orders that command such acts.

2312-2314
2328

486. What must be done to avoid war?

Because of the evils and injustices that all war brings with it, we must do everything reasonably possible to avoid it. To this end it is particularly important to avoid: the accumulation and sale of arms which are not regulated by the legitimate authorities; all forms of economic and social injustice; ethnic and religious discrimination; envy, mistrust, pride and the spirit of revenge. Everything done to overcome these and other disorders contributes to building up peace and avoiding war.

2315-2317
2327-2330

THE SIXTH COMMANDMENT: YOU SHALL NOT COMMIT ADULTERY

487. What responsibility do human persons have in regard to their own sexual identity?

God has created human beings as male and female, equal in personal dignity, and has called them to a vocation of love and of communion. Everyone should accept his or her identity as male or female, recognizing its importance for the whole of the person, its specificity and complementarity.

2331-2336
2392-2393

488. What is chastity?

Chastity means the positive integration of sexuality within the person. Sexuality becomes truly human when it is integrated in a correct

2337-2338

way into the relationship of one person to another. Chastity is a moral virtue, a gift of God, a grace, and a fruit of the Holy Spirit.

489. What is involved in the virtue of chastity?

2339-2341 The virtue of chastity involves an apprenticeship in self-mastery as an expression of human freedom directed towards self-giving. An integral and continuing formation, which is brought about in stages, is necessary to achieve this goal.

490. What are the means that aid the living of chastity?

2340-2347 There are many means at one's disposal: the grace of God, the help of the sacraments, prayer, self-knowledge, the practice of an asceticism adapted to various situations, the exercise of the moral virtues, especially the virtue of temperance which seeks to have the passions guided by reason.

491. In what way is everyone called to live chastity?

2348-2350 As followers of Christ, the model of all chastity, all the baptized are
2394 called to live chastely in keeping with their particular states of life. Some profess virginity or consecrated celibacy which enables them to give themselves to God alone with an undivided heart in a remarkable manner. Others, if they are married live in conjugal chastity, or if unmarried practice chastity in continence.

492. What are the principal sins against chastity?

2351-2359 Grave sins against chastity differ according to their object: adul-
2396 tery, masturbation, fornication, pornography, prostitution, rape, and homosexual acts. These sins are expressions of the vice of lust. These kinds of acts committed against the physical and moral integrity of minors become even more grave.

493. Although it says only "you shall not commit adultery" why does the sixth commandment forbid all sins against chastity?

2336 Although the biblical text of the Decalogue reads "you shall not commit adultery" (Exodus 20:14), the Tradition of the Church comprehensively follows the moral teachings of the Old and New Testaments and considers the sixth commandment as encompassing all sins against chastity.

494. What is the responsibility of civil authority in regard to chastity?

Insofar as it is bound to promote respect for the dignity of the person, civil authority should seek to create an environment conducive to the practice of chastity. It should also enact suitable legislation to prevent the spread of the grave offenses against chastity mentioned above, especially in order to protect minors and those who are the weakest members of society.

2354

495. What are the goods of conjugal love to which sexuality is ordered?

The goods of conjugal love, which for those who are baptized is sanctified by the sacrament of Matrimony, are unity, fidelity, indissolubility, and an openness to the procreation of life.

2360-2361
2397-2398

496. What is the meaning of the conjugal act?

The conjugal act has a twofold meaning: unitive (the mutual self-giving of the spouses) and procreative (an openness to the transmission of life). No one may break the inseparable connection which God has established between these two meanings of the conjugal act by excluding one or the other of them.

2362-2367

497. When is it moral to regulate births?

The regulation of births, which is an aspect of responsible fatherhood and motherhood, is objectively morally acceptable when it is pursued by the spouses without external pressure; when it is practiced not out of selfishness but for serious reasons; and with methods that conform to the objective criteria of morality, that is, periodic continence and use of the infertile periods.

2368-2369
2399

498. What are immoral means of birth control?

Every action—for example, direct sterilization or contraception—is intrinsically immoral which (either in anticipation of the conjugal

2370-2372

act, in its accomplishment or in the development of its natural consequences) proposes, as an end or as a means, to hinder procreation.

499. Why are artificial insemination and artificial fertilization immoral?

2373-2377   They are immoral because they dissociate procreation from the act with which the spouses give themselves to each other and so introduce the domination of technology over the origin and destiny of the human person. Furthermore, heterologous insemination and fertilization with the use of techniques that involve a person other than the married couple infringe upon the right of a child to be born of a father and mother known to him, bound to each other by marriage and having the exclusive right to become parents only through each other.

500. How should children be considered?

2378   A child is a *gift of God*, the supreme gift of marriage. There is no such thing as a right to have children (e.g., "a child at any cost"). But a child does have the right to be the fruit of the conjugal act of its parents as well as the right to be respected as a person from the moment of conception.

501. What can spouses do when they do not have children?

2379   Should the gift of a child not be given to them, after exhausting all legitimate medical options, spouses can show their generosity by way of foster care or adoption or by performing meaningful services for others. In this way they realize a precious spiritual fruitfulness.

502. What are the offenses against the dignity of marriage?

2380-2391   These are: adultery, divorce, polygamy, incest, free unions (cohabita-
2400   tion, concubinage), and sexual acts before or outside of marriage.

THE SEVENTH COMMANDMENT: YOU SHALL NOT STEAL

503. What is set forth by the seventh commandment?

The seventh commandment requires respect for the universal desti-   2401-2402
nation and distribution of goods and the private ownership of them,
as well as respect for persons, their property, and the integrity of creation. The Church also finds in this Commandment the basis for her
social doctrine which involves the correct way of acting in economic,
social and political life, the right and the duty of human labor, justice
and solidarity among nations, and love for the poor.

504. Under what conditions does the right to private property exist?

The right to private property exists provided the property is acquired   2403
or received in a just way and that the universal destination of goods
for the satisfaction of the basic needs of all takes precedence.

505. What is the purpose of private property?

The purpose of private property is to guarantee the freedom and dig-   2404-2406
nity of individual persons by helping them to meet the basic needs of
those in their charge and also of others who are in need.

506. What does the seventh commandment require?

The seventh commandment requires respect for the goods of others   2407
through the practice of justice and charity, temperance and solidarity.   2450-2451
In particular it requires *respect for promises made and contracts agreed to,*
reparation for injustice committed and restitution of stolen goods, and
respect for the *integrity of creation* by the prudent and moderate use
of the mineral, vegetable, and animal resources of the universe with
special attention to those species which are in danger of extinction.

507. What attitude should people have toward animals?

People must treat animals with kindness as creatures of God and   2416-2418
avoid both excessive love for them and an indiscriminate use of them   2457
especially by scientific experiments that go beyond reasonable limits
and entail needless suffering for the animals.

508. What is forbidden by the seventh commandment?

2408-2413 Above all, the seventh commandment forbids theft, which is the tak-
2453-2455 ing or using of another's property against the reasonable will of the
owner. This can be done also by paying unjust wages; by speculation
on the value of goods in order to gain an advantage to the detriment
of others; or by the forgery of checks or invoices. Also forbidden is tax
evasion or business fraud; willfully damaging private or public property; usury; corruption; the private abuse of common goods; work
deliberately done poorly; and waste.

509. What is the content of the social doctrine of the Church?

2419-2423 The social doctrine of the Church is an organic development of the
truth of the Gospel about the dignity of the human person and his
social dimension offering principles for reflection, criteria for judgment, and norms and guidelines for action.

510. When does the Church intervene in social areas?

2420 The Church intervenes by making a moral judgment about economic
2458 and social matters when the fundamental rights of the person, the
common good, or the salvation of souls requires it.

511. How should social and economic life be pursued?

2459 It should be pursued according to its own proper methods within the
sphere of the moral order, at the service of the whole human being
and of the entire human community in keeping with social justice.
Social and economic life should have the human person as its author,
center, and goal.

512. What would be opposed to the social doctrine of the Church?

2424-2425 Opposed to the social doctrine of the Church are economic and social
systems that sacrifice the basic rights of persons or that make profit
their exclusive norm or ultimate end. For this reason the Church
rejects the ideologies associated in modern times with Communism
or with atheistic and totalitarian forms of socialism. But in the practice of capitalism the Church also rejects self centered individual-
ism and an absolute primacy of the laws of the marketplace over
human labor.

513. What is the meaning of work?

Work is both a duty and a right through which human beings col- 2426-2428
laborate with God the Creator. Indeed, by working with commit- 2460-2461
ment and competence we fulfil the potential inscribed in our nature,
honor the Creator's gifts and the talents received from him, provide
for ourselves and for our families, and serve the human community.
Furthermore, by the grace of God, work can be a means of sanctification and collaboration with Christ for the salvation of others.

514. To what type of work does every person have a right?

Access to secure and honest employment must be open to all without 2429
unjust discrimination and with respect for free economic initiative 2433-2434
and fair compensation.

515. What responsibility does the State have in regard to labor?

It is the role of the State to guarantee individual freedom and private 2431
property, as well as a stable currency and efficient public services.
It is also the State's responsibility to oversee and direct the exercise
of human rights in the economic sector. According to circumstances,
society must help citizens to find work.

516. What is the task of business management?

Business managers are responsible for the economic and ecological 2432
effects of their operations. They must consider the good of persons
and not only the increase of profits, even though profits are necessary
to assure investments, the future of the business, employment, and
the good progress of economic life.

517. What are the duties of workers?

They must carry out their work in a conscientious way with compe- 2435
tence and dedication, seeking to resolve any controversies with dialogue. Recourse to a non-violent strike is morally legitimate when it
appears to be the necessary way to obtain a proportionate benefit and
it takes into account the common good.

518. How is justice and solidarity among nations brought about?

2437-2441   On the international level, all nations and institutions must carry out their work in solidarity and subsidiarity for the purpose of eliminating or at least reducing poverty, the inequality of resources and economic potential, economic and social injustices, the exploitation of persons, the accumulation of debts by poor countries, and the perverse mechanisms that impede the development of the less advanced countries.

519. In what way do Christians participate in political and social life?

2442   The lay faithful take part directly in political and social life by animating temporal realities with a Christian spirit and collaborating with all as authentic witnesses of the Gospel and agents of peace and justice.

520. By what is love for the poor inspired?

2443-2449   Love for the poor is inspired by the Gospel of the Beatitudes and by
2462-2463   the example of Jesus in his constant concern for the poor. Jesus said, "Whatever you have done to the least of my brethren, you have done to me" (Matthew 25:40). Love for the poor shows itself through the struggle against material poverty and also against the many forms of cultural, moral, and religious poverty. The spiritual and corporal works of mercy and the many charitable institutions formed throughout the centuries are a concrete witness to the preferential love for the poor which characterizes the disciples of Jesus.

THE EIGHTH COMMANDMENT: YOU SHALL NOT BEAR FALSE WITNESS AGAINST YOUR NEIGHBOR

521. What is one's duty toward the truth?

2464-2470   Every person is called to sincerity and truthfulness in acting and
2504   speaking. Everyone has the duty to seek the truth, to adhere to it and to order one's whole life in accordance with its demands. In Jesus Christ the whole of God's truth has been made manifest. He is *the truth.* Those who follow him live in the Spirit of truth and guard against duplicity, dissimulation, and hypocrisy.

522. How does one bear witness to the truth?

A Christian must bear witness to the truth of the Gospel in every field   2471-2474
of his activity, both public and private, and also if necessary, with the   2505-2506
sacrifice of his very life. Martyrdom is the supreme witness given to
the truth of the faith.

523. What is forbidden by the eighth commandment?

The eighth commandment forbids:
     —*false witness*, *perjury*, and *lying*, the gravity of which is measured   2475-2487
by the truth it deforms, the circumstances, the intentions of the one   2507-2509
who lies, and the harm suffered by its victims;
     —*rash judgment*, *slander*, *defamation* and *calumny* which diminish
or destroy the good reputation and honor to which every person has
a right;
     —*flattery*, *adulation*, or *complaisance*, especially if directed to seri-
ous sins or toward the achievement of illicit advantages.
     A sin committed against truth demands reparation if it has
caused harm to others.

524. What is required by the eighth commandment?

The eighth commandment requires respect for the truth accompa-   2488-2492
nied by the discretion of charity in the field of *communication* and the   2510-2511
imparting of information, where the personal and common good, the
protection of privacy and the danger of scandal must all be taken into
account; in respecting *professional secrets* which must be kept, save in
exceptional cases for grave and proportionate reasons; and also in
respecting *confidences* given under the seal of secrecy.

525. How is one to use the means of social communication?

The information provided by the media must be at the service of the   2493-2499
common good. Its content must be true and—within the limits of jus-   2512
tice and charity—also complete. Furthermore, information must be
communicated honestly and properly with scrupulous respect for
moral laws and the legitimate rights and dignity of the person.

526. What relationship exists between truth, beauty and sacred art?

2500-2503
2513

The truth is beautiful, carrying in itself the splendor of spiritual beauty. In addition to the expression of the truth in words there are other complementary expressions of the truth, most specifically in the beauty of artistic works. These are the fruit both of talents given by God and of human effort. *Sacred art* by being true and beautiful should evoke and glorify the mystery of God made visible in Christ, and lead to the adoration and love of God, the Creator and Savior, who is the surpassing, invisible Beauty of Truth and Love.

THE NINTH COMMANDMENT: YOU SHALL NOT COVET YOUR NEIGHBOR'S WIFE

527. What is required by the ninth commandment?

2514-2516
2528-2530

The ninth commandment requires that one overcome carnal concupiscence in thought and in desire. The struggle against such concupiscence entails purifying the heart and practicing the virtue of temperance.

528. What is forbidden by the ninth commandment?

2517-2519
2531-2532

The ninth commandment forbids cultivating thoughts and desires connected to actions forbidden by the sixth commandment.

529. How does one reach purity of heart?

2520

In the battle against disordered desires the baptized person is able, by the grace of God, to achieve purity of heart through the virtue and gift of chastity, through purity of intention, purity of vision (both exterior and interior), discipline of the imagination and of feelings and by prayer.

530. What are the other requirements for purity?

2521-2527
2533

Purity requires *modesty* which, while protecting the intimate center of the person, expresses the sensitivity of chastity. It guides how one looks at others and behaves toward them in conformity with the dignity of persons and their communion. Purity frees one from widespread eroticism and avoids those things which foster morbid curiosity. Purity also requires a *purification of the social climate* by means of a constant struggle against moral permissiveness which is founded on an erroneous conception of human freedom.

THE TENTH COMMANDMENT: YOU SHALL NOT COVET YOUR NEIGHBOR'S POSSESSIONS

531. What is required and what is forbidden by the tenth commandment?

This commandment, which completes the preceding commandment, requires an interior attitude of respect for the property of others and forbids *greed, unbridled covetousness* for the goods of others, and *envy* which is the sadness one experiences at the sight of another's goods and the immoderate desire to acquire them for oneself. 2534-2540
2551-2554

532. What does Jesus call for in poverty of spirit?

Jesus calls his disciples to prefer him to everything and everyone. Detachment from riches—in the spirit of evangelical poverty—and self-abandonment to divine providence free us from anxiety about the future and prepare us for the blessedness of the "poor in spirit, for theirs is the kingdom of heaven" (Matthew 5:3). 2544-2547
2556

533. What is the greatest human desire?

The greatest desire of the human person is to see God. "I want to see God" is the cry of our whole being. We realize our true and full happiness in the vision and beatitude of the One who created us out of love and draws us to himself with infinite love. 2548-2550
2557

> *"Whoever sees God has obtained all the goods of which he can conceive."* (Saint Gregory of Nyssa)

This icon calls to mind the biblical account of Pentecost.

"When the time for Pentecost was fulfilled, they were all in one place together. And suddenly there came from the sky a noise like a strong driving wind, and it filled the entire house in which they were. Then there appeared to them tongues as of fire, which parted and came to rest on each one of them. And they were all filled with the holy Spirit and began to speak in different tongues, as the Spirit enabled them to proclaim" (Acts 2:1-4).

In this image there comes from the dove, a symbol of the Holy Spirit, a cone of intense light which wraps itself around Mary and the Apostles. This is the light which illumines the minds of the Apostles and gives them the gifts of knowledge, wisdom, and understanding of divine things along with the gifts of piety, fortitude, counsel, and fear of the Lord.

Tongues of fire rest on their heads to show the fullness of God's love which will move them to be preachers of the Gospel to all the nations. This abundance of grace will actually enable the Apostles to be understood by all for the language of charity is universal and accessible to all.

To the barrier which the different languages created among people Pentecost counterpoises the remedy of unity among the nations.

Mary, mother of the Church, the Queen of the Apostles, and the perfect pray-er, is the dominant figure at the center of the icon. It is in the love of the Holy Spirit that the faithful can raise their filial prayer to God in accord with the words of the Apostle:

"As proof that you are children, God sent the spirit of his Son into our hearts, crying out, 'Abba, Father!'" (Galatians 4:6).

Coptic icon of Pentecost. (Used with permission from the Coptic Network, *www.coptic.net*.)

PART FOUR
CHRISTIAN PRAYER

SECTION ONE
PRAYER IN THE CHRISTIAN LIFE

All times are good for prayer. The Church, however, proposes special times to the faithful to stress and nurture continual prayer: morning and evening prayer, prayers before and after meals, the Liturgy of the Hours, the Sunday Eucharist, the rosary, and the feasts of the liturgical year.

This icon portrays some of the major feasts of the liturgical year which mark the prayer of the Church. The representation of the Paschal Mystery, the resurrection and the ascension of Jesus into heaven, is the dominant figure at the center of the icon. This solemn feast is the summit of liturgical prayer and from it all the other feasts, both those of Jesus and Mary, draw their meaning and saving efficacy.

Byzantine icon of the principal liturgical feasts.

534. What is prayer?

Prayer is the raising of one's mind and heart to God, or the petition of good things from him in accord with his will. It is always the gift of God who comes to encounter man. Christian prayer is the personal and living relationship of the children of God with their Father who is infinitely good, with his Son Jesus Christ, and with the Holy Spirit who dwells in their hearts. 2558-2565 2590

CHAPTER ONE
The Revelation of Prayer

535. Why is there a universal call to prayer?

Because through creation God first calls every being from nothingness. Even after the Fall man continues to be capable of recognizing his Creator and retains a desire for the One who has called him into existence. All religions, and the whole history of salvation in particular, bear witness to this human desire for God. It is God first of all, however, who ceaselessly draws every person to the mysterious encounter known as prayer. 2566-2567

THE REVELATION OF PRAYER IN THE OLD TESTAMENT

536. How is Abraham a model of prayer?

Abraham is a model of prayer because he walked in the presence of God, heard and obeyed him. His prayer was a battle of faith because he continued to believe in the fidelity of God even in times of trial. Besides, after having received in his own tent the visit of the Lord who confided his plan to him, Abraham dared to intercede for sinners with bold confidence. 2570-2573 2592

537. How did Moses pray?

The prayer of Moses was typical of contemplative prayer. God, who called to Moses from the burning bush, lingered in conversation with him often and at length, "face to face, like a man with his friend" (Exodus 33:11). In this intimacy with God, Moses attained the strength 2574-2577 2593 to intercede tenaciously for his people: his prayer thus prefigured the intercession of the one mediator, Christ Jesus.

538. In the Old Testament, what relationship do the king and the temple have to prayer?

2578-2580   The prayer of the People of God developed in the shadow of the dwell-
2594   ing place of God—the Ark of the Covenant, then the Temple—under the guidance of their shepherds. Among them there was David, the King "after God's own heart," the shepherd who prayed for his people. His prayer was a model for the prayer of the people because it involved clinging to the divine promise and a trust filled with love for the One who is the only King and Lord.

539. What is the role of prayer in the mission of the prophets?

2581-2584   The prophets drew from prayer the light and strength to exhort the people to faith and to conversion of heart. They entered into great intimacy with God and interceded for their brothers and sisters to whom they proclaimed what they had seen and heard from the Lord. Elijah was the father of the prophets, of those who sought the face of God. On Mount Carmel he achieved the return of the people to the faith, thanks to the intervention of God to whom he prayed: "Answer me, O LORD, answer me" (1 Kings 18:37).

540. What is the importance of the Psalms in prayer?

2579   The Psalms are the summit of prayer in the Old Testament: the
2585-2589   Word of God become the prayer of man. Inseparably both personal
2596-2597   and communal, and inspired by the Holy Spirit, this prayer sings of God's marvelous deeds in creation and in the history of salvation. Christ prayed the Psalms and brought them to fulfillment. Thus they remain an essential and permanent element of the prayer of the Church suited to people of every condition and time.

PRAYER IS FULLY REVEALED AND REALIZED IN JESUS

541. From whom did Jesus learn how to pray?

2599   Jesus, with his human heart, learned how to pray from his mother
2620   and from the Jewish tradition. But his prayer sprang from a more

secret source because he is the eternal Son of God who in his holy humanity offers his perfect filial prayer to his Father.

542. When did Jesus pray?

The Gospel often shows Jesus at prayer. We see him draw apart to pray in solitude, even at night. He prays before the decisive moments of his mission or that of his Apostles. In fact, all his life is a prayer because he is in a constant communion of love with the Father.

2600-2604
2620

543. How did Jesus pray during his Passion?

The prayer of Jesus during his agony in the garden of Gethsemani and his last words on the cross reveal the depth of his filial prayer. Jesus brings to completion the loving plan of the Father and takes upon himself all the anguish of humanity and all the petitions and intercessions of the history of salvation. He presents them to the Father who accepts them and answers them beyond all hope by raising his Son from the dead.

2605-2606
2620

544. How does Jesus teach us to pray?

Jesus teaches us to pray not only with the *Our Father* but also when he prays. In this way he teaches us, in addition to the content, the dispositions necessary for every true prayer: purity of heart that seeks the Kingdom and forgives one's enemies, bold and filial faith that goes beyond what we feel and understand, and watchfulness that protects the disciple from temptation.

2608-2614
2621

545. Why is our prayer efficacious?

Our prayer is efficacious because it is united in faith with the prayer of Jesus. In him Christian prayer becomes a communion of love with the Father. In this way we can present our petitions to God and be heard: "Ask, and you will receive, that your joy may be full" (John 16:24).

2615-2616

546. How did the Virgin Mary pray?

Mary's prayer was characterized by faith and by the generous offering of her whole being to God. The Mother of Jesus is also the new Eve, the "Mother of all the living." She prays to Jesus for the needs of all people.

2617, 2618
2622, 2674
2679

547. Is there a prayer of Mary in the Gospel?

2619   Along with the prayer of Mary at Cana in Galilee, the Gospel gives us the *Magnificat* (Luke 1:46-55) which is the song both of the Mother of God and of the Church, the joyous thanksgiving that rises from the hearts of the poor because their hope is met by the fulfillment of the divine promises.

PRAYER IN THE AGE OF THE CHURCH

548. How did the first Christian community in Jerusalem pray?

2623-2624   At the beginning of the *Acts of the Apostles* it is written that in the first community of Jerusalem, educated in the life of prayer by the Holy Spirit, the faithful "devoted themselves to the teaching of the Apostles and to the communal life, to the breaking of the bread and to the prayers" (Acts 2:42).

549. How does the Holy Spirit intervene in the Church's prayer?

2623, 2625   The Holy Spirit, the interior Master of Christian prayer, forms the Church in the life of prayer and allows her to enter ever more deeply into contemplation of and union with the unfathomable mystery of Christ. The forms of prayer expressed in the apostolic and canonical writings remain normative for Christian prayer.

550. What are the essential forms of Christian prayer?

2643-2644   They are blessing and adoration, the prayer of petition and intercession, thanksgiving and praise. The Eucharist contains and expresses all the forms of prayer.

551. What is "blessing"?

2626-2627   The prayer of blessing is man's response to God's gifts: we bless the
2645   Almighty who first blesses us and fills us with his gifts.

552. How can adoration be defined?

2628   Adoration is the humble acknowledgement by human beings that they are creatures of the thrice-holy Creator.

553. What are the different forms of the prayer of petition?

It can be a petition for pardon or also a humble and trusting petition for all our needs either spiritual or material. The first thing to ask for, however, is the coming of the Kingdom. 2629-2633 2646

554. In what does the prayer of intercession consist?

Intercession consists in asking on behalf of another. It conforms us and unites us to the prayer of Jesus who intercedes with the Father for all, especially sinners. Intercession must extend even to one's enemies. 2634-2636 2647

555. When is thanksgiving given to God?

The Church gives thanks to God unceasingly, above all in celebrating the Eucharist in which Christ allows her to participate in his own thanksgiving to the Father. For the Christian every event becomes a reason for giving thanks. 2637-2638 2648

556. What is the prayer of praise?

Praise is that form of prayer which recognizes most immediately that God is God. It is a completely disinterested prayer: it sings God's praise for his own sake and gives him glory simply because he is. 2639-2643 2649

CHAPTER TWO
The Tradition of Prayer

557. What is the importance of Tradition in regard to prayer?

In the Church it is through living Tradition that the Holy Spirit teaches the children of God how to pray. In fact prayer cannot be reduced to the spontaneous outpouring of an interior impulse; rather it implies contemplation, study and a grasp of the spiritual realities one experiences. 2650-2651

558. What are the sources of Christian prayer?

2652-2662   They are: the *Word of God* which gives us "the surpassing knowledge" of Christ (Philippians 3:8); the *Liturgy of the Church* that proclaims, makes present and communicates the mystery of salvation; the *theological virtues*; and *everyday situations* because in them we can encounter God.

> *"I love you, Lord, and the only grace I ask is to love you eternally.*
> *... My God, if my tongue cannot say in every moment that I love*
> *you, I want my heart to repeat it to you as often as I draw breath."*
> (The Curé of Ars, Saint John Mary Vianney)

THE WAY OF PRAYER

559. In the Church are there different ways of praying?

2663   In the Church there are various ways of praying that are tied to different historical, social and cultural contexts. The Magisterium of the Church has the task of discerning the fidelity of these ways of praying to the tradition of apostolic faith. It is for pastors and catechists to explain their meaning which is always related to Jesus Christ.

560. What is the way of our prayer?

2664
2680-2681   The way of our prayer is Christ because prayer is directed to God our Father but reaches him only if we pray—at least implicitly—in the name of Jesus. His humanity is in effect the only way by which the Holy Spirit teaches us to pray to our Father. Therefore liturgical prayers conclude with the formula: "Through our Lord Jesus Christ."

561. What is the role of the Holy Spirit in prayer?

2670-2672
2680-2681   Since the Holy Spirit is the interior Master of Christian prayer and "we do not know how to pray as we ought" (Rom 8:26), the Church exhorts us to invoke him and implore him on every occasion: "Come, Holy Spirit!"

562. How is Christian prayer Marian?

Because of her singular cooperation with the action of the Holy Spirit, the Church loves to pray to Mary and with Mary, the perfect 'pray-er,' and to "magnify" and invoke the Lord with her. Mary in effect shows us the "Way" who is her Son, the one and only Mediator.

2673-2679
2682

563. How does the Church pray to Mary?

Above all with the *Hail Mary,* the prayer with which the Church asks the intercession of the Virgin. Other Marian prayers are the *Rosary,* the *Akathistos* hymn, the *Paraclesis,* and the hymns and canticles of diverse Christian traditions.

2676-2678
2682

GUIDES FOR PRAYER

564. How are the saints guides for prayer?

The saints are our models of prayer. We also ask them to intercede before the Holy Trinity for us and for the whole world. Their intercession is their most exalted service to God's plan. In the communion of saints, throughout the history of the Church, there have developed different types of *spiritualities* that teach us how to live and to practice the way of prayer.

2683-2684
2692-2693

565. Who can educate us in prayer?

The Christian family is the first place of education in prayer. Daily family prayer is particularly recommended because it is the first witness to the life of prayer in the Church. Catechesis, prayer groups, and "spiritual direction" constitute a school of and a help to prayer.

2685-2690
2694-2695

566. What places are conducive to prayer?

One can pray anywhere but the choice of an appropriate place is not a matter of indifference when it comes to prayer. The church is the proper place for liturgical prayer and Eucharistic adoration. Other places also help one to pray, such as a "prayer corner" at home, a monastery or a shrine.

2691
2696

CHAPTER THREE

The Life of Prayer

567. What times are more suitable for prayer?

2697-2698   Any time is suitable for prayer but the Church proposes to the faith-
2720   ful certain rhythms of praying intended to nourish continual prayer:
morning and evening prayer, prayer before and after meals, the
Liturgy of the Hours, Sunday Eucharist, the Rosary, and feasts of the
liturgical year.

> *"We must remember God more often than we draw breath."*
> (Saint Gregory of Nazianzus)

568. What are the expressions of the life of prayer?

2697-2699   Christian tradition has preserved three forms for expressing and living prayer: vocal prayer, meditation, and contemplative prayer. The
feature common to all of them is the recollection of the heart.

EXPRESSIONS OF PRAYER

569. How can vocal prayer be described?

2700-2704   Vocal prayer associates the body with the interior prayer of the heart.
2722   Even the most interior prayer, however, cannot dispense with vocal
prayer. In any case it must always spring from a personal faith. With
the *Our Father* Jesus has taught us a perfect form of vocal prayer.

570. What is meditation?

2705-2708   Meditation is a prayerful reflection that begins above all in the Word
2723   of God in the Bible. Meditation engages thought, imagination, emo-
tion and desire in order to deepen our faith, convert our heart and
fortify our will to follow Christ. It is a first step toward the union of
love with our Lord.

571. What is contemplative prayer?

Contemplative prayer is a simple gaze upon God in silence and love. It is a gift of God, a moment of pure faith during which the one praying seeks Christ, surrenders himself to the loving will of the Father, and places his being under the action of the Holy Spirit. Saint Teresa of Avila defines contemplative prayer as the intimate sharing of friendship, "in which time is frequently taken to be alone with God who we know loves us."

2709-2719
2724
2739-2741

THE BATTLE OF PRAYER

572. Why is prayer a "battle"?

Prayer is a gift of grace but it always presupposes a determined response on our part because those who pray "battle" against themselves, their surroundings, and especially the Tempter who does all he can to turn them away from prayer. The battle of prayer is inseparable from progress in the spiritual life. We pray as we live because we live as we pray.

2725

573. Are there objections to prayer?

Along with erroneous notions of prayer, many think they do not have the time to pray or that praying is useless. Those who pray can be discouraged in the face of difficulties and apparent lack of success. Humility, trust and perseverance are necessary to overcome these obstacles.

2726-2728
2752-2753

574. What are the difficulties in prayer?

Distraction is a habitual difficulty in our prayer. It takes our attention away from God and can also reveal what we are attached to. Our heart therefore must humbly turn to the Lord. Prayer is often affected by *dryness*. Overcoming this difficulty allows us to cling to the Lord in faith, even without any feeling of consolation. *Acedia* is a form of spiritual laziness due to relaxed vigilance and a lack of custody of the heart.

2729-2733
2754-2755

575. How may we strengthen our filial trust?

2734-2741   Filial trust is tested when we think we are not heard. We must there-
2756   fore ask ourselves if we think God is truly a Father whose will we
seek to fulfill, or simply a means to obtain what we want. If our prayer
is united to that of Jesus, we know that he gives us much more than
this or that gift. We receive the Holy Spirit who transforms our heart.

576. Is it possible to pray always?

2742-2745   Praying is always possible because the time of the Christian is the
2757   time of the risen Christ who remains "with you always" (Mt 28:20).
Prayer and Christian life are therefore inseparable:

> "It is possible to offer frequent and fervent prayer even at the
> market place or strolling alone. It is possible also in your place of
> business, while buying or selling, or even while cooking." (Saint
> John Chrysostom)

577. What is the prayer of the *Hour* of Jesus?

2604   It is called the priestly prayer of Jesus at the Last Supper. Jesus, the High
2746-2751   Priest of the New Covenant, addresses it to his Father when the *hour*
2758   of his sacrifice, the *hour* of his "passing over" to him is approaching.

THE LORD'S PRAYER: "OUR FATHER"

Our Father

Our Father who art in heaven,
hallowed be thy name.
Thy kingdom come.
Thy will be done on earth, as it is
in heaven.
Give us this day our daily bread,
and forgive us our trespasses,
   as we forgive those who trespass
   against us,
and lead us not into temptation,
but deliver us from evil.

Pater Noster

Pater noster qui es in cælis:
sanctificétur Nomen Tuum;
advéniat Regnum Tuum;
fiat volúntas Tua,
sicut in cælo, et in terra.
Panem nostrum
cotidiánum da nobis hódie;
et dimítte nobis débita nostra,
sicut et nos
dimíttimus debitóribus nostris;
et ne nos indúcas in tentatiónem;
sed líbera nos a Malo.

"He was praying in a certain place, and when he had finished, one of his disciples said to him 'Lord, teach us to pray'" (Luke 11:1). Jesus responded by teaching them the *Our Father.*

The disciples, who had experience with Jewish prayer at the time, were greatly struck by the singular character of the prayer of their Master. Jesus actually was in continual prayer (cf. Luke 5:16). The most important moments of his life were accompanied by prayer. Jesus prayed at his baptism in the Jordan (Luke 3:21), before calling the Apostles (Luke 6:12), and before his transfiguration (Luke 9:28). He prayed for the faith of Peter (Luke 22:31-32) and for the sending of the Holy Spirit (John 14:15-17). He prayed before raising Lazarus (John 11:41) and at his triumphant entry into Jerusalem (John 12:27). He prayed to his Father for his own glorification at the Last Supper (John 17:1-5), for his disciples (John 17:6-19), and for all believers (John 17:20-26). He prayed before his Passion (Luke 22:39-46) and at the moment of his death he prayed for his enemies (Luke 23:24).

The prayer of Jesus was addressed to the Father in a dialog of obedience which gave life to his mission: "My food is to do the will of the one who sent me and to finish his work" (John 4:34). This intimate communion with the Father is the source of joy and praise: "I give praise to you, Father, Lord of heaven and earth. . . . All things have been handed over to me by my Father. No one knows the Son except the Father, and no one knows the Father except the Son and anyone to whom the Son wishes to reveal him" (Matthew 11:25, 27).

Prayer to the Father was the life breath of his earthly existence. He came to dwell in our midst but Jesus did not leave the house of the Father because he kept communion with him in prayer. On the other hand, however, this filial intimacy became a merciful and saving closeness for his brothers right up to the supreme sacrifice of the cross.

The prayer of Jesus continues still today (cf. Hebrews 7:25). In the Eucharistic liturgy, Christ the High Priest offers to the Father his redeeming sacrifice. He offers it in communion with his body which is the Church. Every prayer of ours is raised to the Father "through Christ our Lord." It is this prayer of Christ which sustains all our prayers, those spoken and those in the heart. When the Church prays it, it is the Son who embraces the knees of the Father. The prayer of the sons ascends to the Father through the voice of the First Born. The arms raised up in invocation, praise, and supplication are millions but the voice is one alone, that of the Son.

This painting depicts Jesus at prayer in Gethsemane. He accepts the bitter cup of his Passion in an act of supreme obedience to the Father for the salvation of mankind.

El Greco, *Prayer of Jesus in the Garden*, Museum of Art, Toledo, Ohio. (Used with permission of the Toledo Museum of Art. Purchased with funds from the Libbey Endowment, Gift of Edward Drummond Libbery, 1946.5.)

578. What is the origin of the *Our Father*?

Jesus taught us this Christian prayer for which there is no substitute, the *Our Father*, on the day on which one of his disciples saw him praying and asked him, "Lord, teach us to pray" (Luke 11:1). The Church's liturgical tradition has always used the text of Saint Matthew (6:9-13).

2759-2760
2773

"THE SUMMARY OF THE WHOLE GOSPEL"

579. What is the place of the *Our Father* in the Scriptures?

The *Our Father* is the "summary of the whole Gospel" (Tertullian), "the perfect prayer" (Saint Thomas Aquinas). Found in the middle of the Sermon on the Mount (Matthew 5-7), it presents in the form of prayer the essential content of the Gospel.

2761-2764
2774

580. Why is it called the "Lord's Prayer"?

The *Our Father* is called the "Oratio Dominica," that is, the Lord's Prayer because it was taught to us by the Lord Jesus himself.

2765-2766
2775

581. What place does the *Our Father* have in the prayer of the Church?

The *Lord's Prayer* is the prayer of the Church *par excellence*. It is "handed on" in Baptism to signify the new birth of the children of God into the divine life. The full meaning of the *Our Father* is revealed in the Eucharist since its petitions are based on the mystery of salvation already accomplished, petitions that will be fully heard at the coming of the Lord. The *Our Father* is an integral part of the Liturgy of the Hours.

2767-2772
2776

"OUR FATHER WHO ART IN HEAVEN"

582. Why can we dare to draw near to God in full confidence?

Because Jesus, our Redeemer, brings us into the Father's presence and his Spirit makes us his children. We are thus able to pray the *Our Father* with simple and filial trust, with joyful assurance and humble boldness, with the certainty of being loved and heard.

2777-2778
2797

583. How is it possible to address God as "Father"?

2779-2785 We can invoke the "Father" because the Son of God made man has
2789 revealed him to us and because his Spirit makes him known to us.
2798-2800 The invocation, Father, lets us enter into his mystery with an ever new
sense of wonder and awakens in us the desire to act as his children.
When we pray the Lord's Prayer, we are therefore aware of our being
sons of the Father in the Son.

584. Why do we say "our" Father?

2786-2790 "Our" expresses a totally new relationship with God. When we pray
2801 to the Father, we adore and glorify him with the Son and the Holy
Spirit. In Christ we are "his" people and he is "our" God now and
for eternity. In fact, we also say "our" Father because the Church of
Christ is the communion of a multitude of brothers and sisters who
have but "one heart and mind" (Acts 4:32).

585. With what spirit of communion and mission do we pray to God as "our" Father?

2791-2793 Since praying to "our" Father is a common blessing for the baptized,
2801 we feel an urgent summons to join in Jesus' prayer for the unity of
his disciples. To pray the "Our Father" is to pray with all people and
for all people that they may know the one true God and be gathered
into unity.

586. What does the phrase "Who art in heaven" mean?

2794-2796 This biblical expression does not indicate a place but a way of being:
2802 God transcends everything. The expression refers to the majesty, the
holiness of God, and also to his presence in the hearts of the just.
Heaven, or the Father's house, constitutes our true homeland toward
which we are moving in hope while we are still on earth. "Hidden
with Christ in God" (Col 3:3), we live already in this homeland.

THE SEVEN PETITIONS

587. What is the structure of the Lord's Prayer?

It contains seven petitions made to God the Father. The first three, more God-centered, draw us toward him for his glory; it is characteristic of love to think first of the beloved. These petitions suggest in particular what we ought to ask of him: the sanctification of his Name, the coming of his Kingdom, and the fulfillment of his will. The last four petitions present to the Father of mercies our wretchedness and our expectations. They ask him to feed us, to forgive us, to sustain us in temptations, and to free us from the Evil One.

2803-2806
2857

588. What does "Hallowed be thy Name" mean?

To hallow or make holy the Name of God is above all a prayer of praise that acknowledges God as holy. In fact, God revealed his holy Name to Moses and wanted *his* people to be consecrated for him as a holy nation in which he would dwell.

2807-2812
2858

589. How is the Name of God made holy in us and in the world?

To make holy the Name of God, who calls us "to holiness" (1 Thessalonians 4:7) is to desire that our baptismal consecration animate our whole life. In addition, it is to ask—with our lives and our prayers—that the Name of God be known and blessed by every man.

2813-2815

590. What does the Church ask for when she prays "Thy Kingdom come"?

The Church prays for the final coming of the Kingdom of God through Christ's return in glory. The Church prays also that the Kingdom of God increase from now on through people's sanctification in the Spirit and through their commitment to the service of justice and peace in keeping with the Beatitudes. This petition is the cry of the Spirit and the Bride: "Come, Lord Jesus" (Revelation 22:20).

2816-2821
2859

591. Why pray "Thy will be done on earth as it is in heaven"?

The will of the Father is that "all men . . . be saved" (1 Timothy 2:4). For this Jesus came: to perfectly fulfill the saving will of his Father. We pray God our Father to unite our will to that of his Son after the exam-

2822-2827
2860

ple of the Blessed Virgin Mary and the saints. We ask that this loving plan be fully realized on earth as it is already in heaven. It is through prayer that we can discern "what is the will of God" (Romans 12:2) and have the "steadfastness to do it" (Hebrews 10:36).

592. What is the sense of the petition "Give us this day our daily bread"?

2828-2834   Asking God with the filial trust of children for the daily nourishment
2861   which is necessary for us all we recognize how good God is, beyond all goodness. We ask also for the grace to know how to act so that justice and solidarity may allow the abundance of some to remedy the needs of others.

593. What is the specifically Christian sense of this petition?

2835-2837   Since "man does not live by bread alone but by every word that comes
2861   from the mouth of God" (Matthew 4:4), this petition equally applies to hunger for the *Word of God* and for the *Body of Christ* received in the Eucharist as well as hunger for the Holy Spirit. We ask this with complete confidence for *this day*—God's "today"—and this is given to us above all in the Eucharist which anticipates the banquet of the Kingdom to come.

594. Why do we say "Forgive us our trespasses as we forgive those who trespass against us"?

2838-2839   By asking God the Father to pardon us, we acknowledge before him
2862   that we are sinners. At the same time we proclaim his mercy because in his Son and through the sacraments "we have redemption, the forgiveness of sins" (Colossians 1:14). Still our petition will be answered only if we for our part have forgiven first.

595. How is forgiveness possible?

2840-2845   Mercy can penetrate our hearts only if we ourselves learn how to for-
2862   give—even our enemies. Now even if it seems impossible for us to satisfy this requirement, the heart that offers itself to the Holy Spirit can, like Christ, love even to love's extreme; it can turn injury into compassion and transform hurt into intercession. Forgiveness participates in the divine mercy and is a high-point of Christian prayer.

596. What does "Lead us not into temptation" mean?

We ask God our Father not to leave us alone and in the power of   2846-2849
temptation. We ask the Holy Spirit to help us know how to discern, on   2863
the one hand, between a *trial* that makes us grow in goodness and a
temptation that leads to sin and death and, on the other hand, between
being tempted and *consenting* to temptation. This petition unites us to
Jesus who overcame temptation by his prayer. It requests the grace of
vigilance and of final perseverance.

597. Why do we conclude by asking "But deliver us from evil"?

"Evil" indicates the person of Satan who opposes God and is "the   2850-2854
deceiver of the whole world" (Revelation 12:9). Victory over the devil   2864
has already been won by Christ. We pray, however, that the human
family be freed from Satan and his works. We also ask for the precious gift of peace and the grace of perseverance as we wait for the
coming of Christ who will free us definitively from the Evil One.

598. What is the meaning of the final *Amen*?

"At the end of the prayer, you say 'Amen' and thus you ratify by   2855-2856
this word that means 'so be it' all that is contained in this prayer   2865
that God has taught us." (Saint Cyril of Jerusalem)

The angels are creatures of God. A part of them remained and remain faithful to him, in his presence, his service, and the service of the Church; and they are united with all the saved in the glory of heaven.

As in the vision of Jacob's ladder—"God's messengers were going up and down on it" (Genesis 28:12)—the angels are energetic and tireless messengers who connect heaven to earth. Between God and mankind there is not silence or a lack of communication but a continual conversation, a ceaseless personal exchange. Men, to whom this communication is addressed, have to sharpen their spiritual ear to hear and understand this angelic language which prompts good words, holy sentiments, acts of mercy, charitable behavior, and edifying relationships.

It is this that we ask of our guardian angel in that well known prayer of popular Catholic devotion:

"Angel of God, my guardian dear,

To whom God's love commits me here,

Ever this day be at my side

To light, to guard, to rule, and guide. Amen."

The image presented here portrays a group of apterous angels (without wings) who pray by singing. They are dressed in sumptuous sacred vestments to indicate that they are discharging a solemn liturgical action. Indeed the angels, besides being messengers of God who are sent to declare his sovereign will to men, perform also the service of praising the Lord in the eternal liturgy of heaven (cf. Revelation 8:2).

Jan Van Eyck, *Angelic Singers*, Polyptych in the Cathedral of Gand. (Photo credit: Erich Lessing/Art Resource, NY.)

APPENDIX

A. COMMON PRAYERS
B. FORMULAS OF CATHOLIC DOCTRINE

A. COMMON PRAYERS

THE SIGN OF THE CROSS
In the name of the Father
and of the Son
and of the Holy Spirit. Amen.

SIGNUM CRUCIS
In nómine Patris
et Fílii
et Spíritus Sancti. Amen.

**GLORY BE TO
THE FATHER**
Glory be to the Father
and to the Son
and to the Holy Spirit,
as it was in the beginning
is now, and ever shall be
world without end. Amen.

GLORIA PATRI
Glória Patri
et Fílio
et Spirítui Sancto.
Sicut erat in princípio,
et nunc et semper
et in sæ´cula sæculórum. Amen.

THE HAIL MARY
Hail, Mary, full of grace,
the Lord is with thee.
Blessed art thou among women
and blessed is the fruit of thy
    womb, Jesus.
Holy Mary, Mother of God,
pray for us sinners,
now and at the hour of
    our death.
Amen.

AVE, MARIA
Ave, María, grátia plena,
Dóminus tecum.
Benedícta tu in muliéribus,
et benedíctus fructus ventris
    tui, Iesus.
Sancta María, Mater Dei,
ora pro nobis peccatóribus,
nunc et in hora mortis nostræ.
    Amen.

ANGEL OF GOD
Angel of God,
my guardian dear,
to whom God's love commits
    me here,
ever this day be at my side,
to light and guard, to rule and guide.
Amen.

ANGELE DEI
Ángele Dei,
qui custos es mei,
me, tibi commíssum pietáte supérna,
illúmina, custódi,
rege et gubérna.
    Amen.

ETERNAL REST
Eternal rest grant unto them, O Lord,
and let perpetual light shine
    upon them.
May they rest in peace. Amen.

REQUIEM ÆTERNAM
Réquiem ætérnam dona eis, Dómine,
et lux perpétua lúceat eis.
Requiéscant in pace. Amen.

THE ANGELUS

V. The Angel of the Lord declared unto Mary.
R. And she conceived of the Holy Spirit.

Hail, Mary, full of grace, the Lord is with thee.
Blessed art thou among women, and blessed is the fruit of thy womb, Jesus.
Holy Mary, Mother of God, pray for us sinners, now and at the hour of our death. Amen.

V. Behold the handmaid of the Lord.
R. Be it done unto me according to thy word.
Hail Mary.

V. And the Word was made flesh.
R. And dwelt among us.
Hail Mary.

V. Pray for us, O holy Mother of God.
R. That we may be made worthy of the promises of Christ.

Let us pray;
Pour forth, we beseech thee, O Lord, thy grace into our hearts; that we, to whom the Incarnation of Christ, thy Son, was made known by the message of an angel, may by his Passion and Cross be brought to the glory of his Resurrection. Through the same Christ, our Lord. Amen.

ANGELUS DOMINI

Ángelus Dómini nuntiávit Maríæ.
Et concépit de Spíritu Sancto.
Ave, María . . .

Ecce ancílla Dómini.
Fiat mihi secúndum verbum tuum.
Ave, María . . .

Et Verbum caro factum est.
Et habitávit in nobis.
Ave, María . . .

Ora pro nobis, sancta Dei génetrix.
Ut digni efficiámur promissiónibus Christi.

Orémus.
Grátiam tuam, quǽsumus, Dómine, méntibus nostris infúnde; ut qui, Ángelo nuntiánte, Christi Fílii tui incarnatiónem cognóvimus, per passiónem eius et crucem, ad resurrectiónis glóriam perducámur.
Per eúndem Christum Dóminum nostrum. Amen.

Glória Patri . . .

REGINA CAELI

Queen of heaven, rejoice, alleluia.
The Son whom you merited to bear, alleluia,
has risen as he said, alleluia.
Pray for us to God, alleluia.
Rejoice and be glad, O Virgin Mary, alleluia!
For the Lord has truly risen, alleluia.

REGINA CÆLI

Regína cæli lætáre,
allelúia.
Quia quem meruísti portáre,
allelúia.
Resurréxit, sicut dixit,
allelúia.
Ora pro nobis Deum,
allelúia.

Let us pray;
O God, who through the resurrection
of your Son, our Lord Jesus Christ,
did vouchsafe to give joy to the world;
grant, we beseech you, that through
his Mother, the Virgin Mary, we may
obtain the joys of everlasting life.
Through the same Christ our Lord.
Amen.

Gaude et lætáre, Virgo María,
    allelúia.
Quia surréxit Dóminus vere,
    allelúia.

Orémus.
Deus, qui per resurrectiónem Fílii tui
Dómini nostri Iesu Christi mundum
lætificáre dignátus es, præsta,
quæ´sumus, ut per eius Genetrícem
Vírginem Maríam perpétuæ
capiámus gáudia vitæ.
Per Christum Dóminum nostrum.
Amen.

HAIL, HOLY QUEEN

Hail, Holy Queen, Mother of Mercy,
our life, our sweetness and our hope.
To thee do we cry,
poor banished children of Eve.
To thee do we send up our sighs,
mourning and weeping in this valley
    of tears.
Turn then, most gracious advocate,
thine eyes of mercy toward us,
and after this exile
show unto us the blessed fruit of thy
    womb, Jesus.
O clement, O loving,
O sweet Virgin Mary.

SALVE, REGINA

Salve, Regína,
Mater misericórdiæ,
vita, dulcédo et spes nostra, salve.
Ad te clamámus,
éxsules fílii Evæ.
Ad te suspirámus geméntes et flentes
in hac lacrimárum valle.
Eia ergo, advocáta nostra,
illos tuos misericórdes óculos ad
    nos convérte.
Et Iesum benedíctum fructum
    ventris tui,
nobis, post hoc exsílium, osténde.
O clemens, o pia, o dulcis
    Virgo María!

THE MAGNIFICAT

My soul proclaims the greatness of
    the Lord,
my spirit rejoices in God my Savior,
for he has looked with favor on his
    lowly servant.
From this day all generations will
    call me blessed:
the Almighty has done great things
    for me,
and holy is his Name.
He has mercy on those who fear him
in every generation.
He has shown the strength of
    his arm,

MAGNIFICAT

Magníficat ánima mea Dóminum,
et exsultávit spíritus meus in Deo
    salvatóre meo,
quia respéxit humilitátem
    ancíllæ suæ.
Ecce enim ex hoc beátam me dicent
    omnes generatiónes,
quia fecit mihi magna, qui potens est,
et sanctum nomen eius,
et misericórdia eius in progénies et
    progénies timéntibus eum.
Fecit poténtiam in bráchio suo,
dispérsit supérbos mente cordis sui;
depósuit poténtes de sede
et exaltávit húmiles.

he has scattered the proud in
their conceit.
He has cast down the mighty from
their thrones,
and has lifted up the lowly.
He has filled the hungry with
good things,
and the rich he has sent away empty.
He has come to the help of his
servant Israel
for he has remembered his promise
of mercy,
the promise he made to our fathers,
to Abraham and his children forever.
Glory to the Father and to the Son
and to the Holy Spirit,
as it was in the beginning, is now,
and will be forever. Amen.

Esuriéntes implévit bonis
et dívites dimísit inánes.
Suscépit Ísrael púerum suum,
recordátus misericórdiæ,
sicut locútus est ad patres nostros,
Ábraham et sémini eius in sǽcula.
Glória Patri et Fílio
et Spirítui Sancto.
Sicut erat in princípio, et nunc
et semper,
et in sǽcula sæculórum.
Amen.

UNDER YOUR PROTECTION

We fly to thy protection, O holy
Mother of God.
Despise not our petitions in
our necessities,
but deliver us always from
all dangers
O glorious and blessed Virgin.

SUB TUUM PRÆSIDIUM

Sub tuum præsídium confúgimus,
sancta Dei Génetrix;
nostras deprecatiónes ne despícias
in necessitátibus;
sed a perículis cunctis líbera
nos semper,
Virgo gloriósa et benedícta.

THE BENEDICTUS

Blessed be the Lord, the God
of Israel;
he has come to his people and set
them free.
He has raised up for us a
mighty savior,
born of the house of his
servant David.
Through his holy prophets he
promised of old
that he would save us from
our enemies,
from the hands of all who hate us.
He promised to show mercy to
our fathers
and to remember his holy covenant.
This was the oath he swore to our
father Abraham:

BENEDICTUS

Benedíctus Dóminus, Deus Ísrael,
quia visitávit et fecit redemptiónem
plebi suæ,
et eréxit cornu salútis nobis
in domo David púeri sui,
sicut locútus est per os sanctórum,
qui a sǽculo sunt, prophetárum eius,
salútem ex inimícis nostris
et de manu ómnium, qui
odérunt nos;
ad faciéndam misericórdiam cum
pátribus nostris
et memorári testaménti sui sancti,
iusiurándum, quod iurávit ad
Ábraham patrem nostrum,
datúrum se nobis,
ut sine timóre, de manu inimicórum
liberáti,
serviámus illi

to set us free from the hands of
  our enemies,
free to worship him without fear,
holy and righteous in his sight all the
  days of our life.
You, my child, shall be called the
  prophet of the Most High;
for you will go before the Lord to
  prepare his way,
to give his people knowledge
  of salvation
by the forgiveness of their sins.
In the tender compassion of our God
the dawn from on high shall break
  upon us,
to shine on those who dwell in
  darkness and the shadow of death,
and to guide our feet into the way
  of peace.
Glory to the Father and to the Son
  and to the Holy Spirit,
as it was in the beginning, is now,
  and will be forever. Amen.

in sanctitáte et iustítia coram ipso
  ómnibus diébus nostris.
Et tu, puer, prophéta Altíssimi
  vocáberis:
præíbis enim ante fáciem Dómini
  paráre vias eius,
ad dandam sciéntiam salútis
  plebi eius
in remissiónem peccatórum eórum,
per víscera misericórdiæ Dei nostri,
in quibus visitábit nos óriens ex alto,
illumináre his, qui in ténebris et in
  umbra mortis sedent,
ad dirigéndos pedes nostros in
  viam pacis.
Glória Patri et Fílio
et Spirítui Sancto.
Sicut erat in princípio, et nunc,
  et semper,
et in sǽcula sæculórum. Amen.

TE DEUM

You are God: we praise you;
You are God: we acclaim you;
You are the eternal Father:
All creation worships you.
To you all angels, all the powers
  of heaven,
Cherubim and Seraphim, sing in
  endless praise:
Holy, holy, holy, Lord, God of power
  and might,
Heaven and earth are full of
  your glory.
The glorious company of apostles
  praise you.
The noble fellowship of prophets
  praise you.
The white-robed army of martyrs
  praise you.
Throughout the world the holy
  Church acclaims you:
Father, of majesty unbounded,
Your true and only Son, worthy of
  all worship,

TE DEUM

Te Deum laudámus:
  te Dóminum confitémur.
Te ætérnum Patrem,
  omnis terra venerátur.
tibi omnes ángeli,
  tibi cæli et univérsæ potestátes:
tibi chérubim et séraphim
  incessábili voce proclámant:
Sanctus, Sanctus, Sanctus,
  Dóminus Deus Sábaoth.
Pleni sunt cæli et terra
  maiestátis glóriæ tuæ.
Te gloriósus
  apostolórum chorus,
te prophetárum
  laudábilis númerus,
te mártyrum candidátus
  laudat exércitus.
Te per orbem terrárum
  sancta confitétur Ecclésia,
Patrem imménsæ maiestátis;
venerándum tuum verum
  et únicum Fílium;

And the Holy Spirit, advocate
  and guide.
You, Christ, are the king of glory,
The eternal Son of the Father.
When you became man to set us free
You did not spurn the
  Virgin's womb.
You overcame the sting of death,
And opened the kingdom of heaven
  to all believers.
You are seated at God's right hand in
  glory.
We believe that you will come, and
  be our judge.
Come then, Lord, and help
  your people,
Bought with the price of your
  own blood,
And bring us with your saints
To glory everlasting.
Save your people, Lord, and bless
  your inheritance.
Govern and uphold them now
  and always.
Day by day we bless you.
We praise your name forever.
Keep us today, Lord, from all sin.
Have mercy on us, Lord, have mercy.
Lord, show us your love and mercy;
For we put our trust in you.
In you, Lord, is our hope:
And we shall never hope in vain.

Sanctum quoque
  Paráclitum Spíritum.
Tu rex glóriæ, Christe.
Tu Patris sempitérnus es Fílius.
Tu, ad liberándum susceptúrus
  hóminem, non horruísti
  Vírginis úterum.
Tu, devícto mortis acúleo,
  aperuísti credéntibus
  regna cælórum.
Tu ad déxteram Dei sedes,
  in glória Patris.
Iudex créderis esse ventúrus.
Te ergo quæ´sumus,
  tuis fámulis súbveni,
  quos pretióso sánguine redemísti.
Ætérna fac cum sanctis tuis
  in glória numerári.
Salvum fac pópulum tuum, Dómine,
  et bénedic hereditáti tuæ.
Et rege eos, et extólle illos
  usque in ætérnum.
Per síngulos dies benedícimus te;
et laudámus nomen tuum
  in sæ´culum, et in sæ´culum
  sæ´culi.
Dignáre, Dómine,
  die isto sine peccáto nos custodíre.
Miserére nostri, Dómine,
  miserére nostri.
Fiat misericórdia tua,
  Dómine, super nos,
quemádmodum sperávimus in te.
In te, Dómine, sperávi:
  non confúndar in ætérnum.

COME, CREATOR SPIRIT

Come, Holy Spirit, Creator come,
From your bright heavenly throne!
Come, take possession of our souls,
And make them all your own.
You who are called the Paraclete,
Best gift of God above,
The living spring, the living fire,
Sweet unction, and true love!
You who are sevenfold in your grace,
Finger of God's right hand,
His promise, teaching little ones

VENI, CREATOR SPIRITUS

Veni, creátor Spíritus,
mentes tuórum vísita,
imple supérna grátia,
quæ tu creásti péctora.
Qui díceris Paráclitus,
altíssimi donum Dei,
fons vivus, ignis, cáritas,
et spiritális únctio.
Tu septifórmis múnere,
dígitus patérnæ déxteræ,
tu rite promíssum Patris,

To speak and understand!
O guide our minds with your
    blessed light,
With love our hearts inflame,
And with your strength which
    never decays
Confirm our mortal frame.
Far from us drive our hellish foe
True peace unto us bring,
And through all perils guide us safe
Beneath your sacred wing.
Through you may we the
    Father know,
Through you the eternal Son
And you the Spirit of them both
Thrice-blessed three in one.
All glory to the Father be,
And to the risen Son;
The same to you, O Paraclete,
While endless ages run. Amen.

sermóne ditans gúttura.
Accénde lumen sénsibus,
infúnde amórem córdibus,
infírma nostri córporis
virtúte firmans pérpeti.
Hostem repéllas lóngius
pacémque dones prótinus;
ductóre sic te præ´vio
vitémus omne nóxium.
Per Te sciámus da Patrem
noscámus atque Fílium,
teque utriúsque Spíritum
credámus omni témpore.
Deo Patri sit glória,
et Fílio, qui a mórtuis
surréxit, ac Paráclito,
in sæculórum sæ´cula. Amen.

COME, HOLY SPIRIT

Come, Holy Spirit, come!
And from your celestial home
Shed a ray of light divine!
Come, Father of the poor!
Come, source of all our store!
Come, within our bosoms shine.
You, of comforters the best;
You, the soul's most welcome guest;
Sweet refreshment here below;
In our labor, rest most sweet;
Grateful coolness in the heat;
Solace in the midst of woe.
O most blessed Light divine,
Shine within these hearts of yours,
And our inmost being fill!
Where you are not, we have naught,
Nothing good in deed or thought,
Nothing free from taint of ill.
Heal our wounds, our
    strength renew;
On our dryness pour your dew;
Wash the stains of guilt away:
Bend the stubborn heart and will;
Melt the frozen, warm the chill;
Guide the steps that go astray.
On the faithful, who adore

VENI, SANCTE SPIRITUS

Veni, Sancte Spíritus,
et emítte cæ´litus
lucis tuæ rádium.
Veni, pater páuperum,
veni, dator múnerum,
veni, lumen córdium.
Consolátor óptime,
dulcis hospes ánimæ,
dulce refrigérium.
In labóre réquies,
in æstu tempéries,
in fletu solácium.
O lux beatíssima,
reple cordis íntima
tuórum fidélium.
Sine tuo númine,
nihil est in hómine
nihil est innóxium.
Lava quod est sórdidum,
riga quod est áridum,
sana quod est sáucium.
Flecte quod est rígidum,
fove quod est frígidum,
rege quod est dévium.
Da tuis fidélibus,
in te confidéntibus,

And confess you, evermore
In your sevenfold gift descend:
Give them virtue's sure reward;
Give them your salvation, Lord;
Give them joys that never end.

sacrum septenárium.
Da virtútis méritum,
da salútis éxitum,
da perénne gáudium. Amen.

ANIMA CHRISTI

Soul of Christ, be my sanctification.
Body of Christ, be my salvation.
Blood of Christ, fill all my veins.
Water of Christ's side, wash out
    my stains.
Passion of Christ, my comfort be.
O good Jesu, listen to me.
In Thy wounds I fain would hide,
N'er to be parted from Thy side,
Guard me, should the foe assail me.
Call me when my life shall fail me.
Bid me come to Thee above,
With Thy saints to sing Thy love,
World without end. Amen.

ANIMA CHRISTI

Ánima Christi, sanctífica me.
Corpus Christi, salva me.
Sanguis Christi, inébria me.
Aqua láteris Christi, lava me.
Pássio Christi, confórta me.
O bone Iesu, exáudi me.
Intra tua vúlnera abscónde me.
Ne permíttas me separári a te.
Ab hoste malígno defénde me.
In hora mortis meæ voca me.
Et iube me veníre ad te,
ut cum Sanctis tuis laudem te
in sǽcula sæculórum. Amen.

MEMORARE

Remember, O most gracious Virgin
Mary, that never was it known that
anyone who fled to thy protection,
implored thy help, or sought thy
intercession, was left unaided.
Inspired by this confidence I fly
unto thee, O Virgin of virgins, my
Mother. To thee do I come, before
thee I stand, sinful and sorrowful.
O Mother of the Word Incarnate,
despise not my petitions, but in thy
mercy hear and answer me. Amen.

MEMORARE

Memoráre, o piíssima Virgo
María, non esse audítum a sǽculo,
quemquam ad tua curréntem
præsídia, tua imploróntem auxília,
tua peténtem suffrágia, esse
derelíctum. Ego tali animátus
confidéntia, ad te, Virgo Vírginum,
Mater, curro, ad te vénio, coram te
gemens peccátor assísto. Noli, Mater
Verbi, verba mea despícere; sed áudi
propítia et exáudi. Amen.

THE ROSARY

The Joyful Mysteries
(recited Monday and Saturday)
1. The Annunciation
2. The Visitation
3. The Nativity
4. The Presentation
5. The Finding in the Temple

The Mysteries of Light
(recited Thursday)
1. The Baptism of Jesus
2. The Wedding Feast of Cana
3. The Proclamation of the Kingdom, with the call to Conversion
4. The Transfiguration
5. The Institution of the Eucharist

The Sorrowful Mysteries
(recited Tuesday and Friday)
1. The Agony in the Garden
2. The Scourging at the Pillar
3. The Crowning with Thorns
4. The Carrying of the Cross
5. The Crucifixion

The Glorious Mysteries
(recited Wednesday and Sunday)
1. The Resurrection
2. The Ascension
3. The Descent of the Holy Spirit
4. The Assumption
5. The Coronation of Mary Queen of Heaven and Earth

Prayer Concluding the Rosary
Hail, Holy Queen, etc. as above
V. Pray for us, O holy Mother of God.
R. That we may be made worthy of the promises of Christ.

ROSARIUM

Mystéria gaudiósa
(in feria secunda et sabbato)
1. Annuntiátio.
2. Visitátio.
3. Natívitas.
4. Præsentátio.
5. Invéntio in Templo.

Mystéria luminósa
(in feria quinta)
1. Baptísma apud Iordánem.
2. Autorevelátio apud Cananénse matrimónium.
3. Regni Dei proclamátio coniúncta cum invitaménto ad conversiónem.
4. Transfigurátio.
5. Eucharístiæ Institútio.

Mystéria dolorósa
(in feria tertia et feria sexta)
1. Agonía in Hortu.
2. Flagellátio.
3. Coronátio Spinis.
4. Baiulátio Crucis.
5. Crucifíxio et Mors.

Mystéria gloriósa
(in feria quarta et Dominica)
1. Resurréctio.
2. Ascénsio.
3. Descénsus Spíritus Sancti.
4. Assúmptio.
5. Coronátio in Cælo.

Oratio ad finem Rosarii dicenda
Ora pro nobis, sancta Dei génetrix.
Ut digni efficiámur promissiónibus Christi.

Let us pray.
O God, whose only-begotten Son,
by his life, death and resurrection,
has purchased for us the rewards of
eternal life, grant, we beseech thee,
that meditating on these mysteries of
the most holy Rosary of the Blessed
Virgin Mary, we may imitate what
they contain and obtain what they
promise, through the same Christ our
Lord. Amen.

Orémus.
Deus, cuius Unigénitus per vitam,
mortem et resurrectiónem suam
nobis salútis ætérnæ præ´mia
comparávit, concéde, quæ´sumus:
ut hæc mystéria sacratíssimo beátæ
Maríæ Vírginis Rosário recoléntes,
et imitémur quod cóntinent, et
quod promíttunt assequámur. Per
Christum Dóminum nostrum. Amen.

COPTIC INCENSE PRAYER

O King of peace, give us your peace
and pardon our sins. Dismiss the
enemies of the Church and protect
her so that she never fail. Emmanuel
our God is in our midst in the glory
of the Father and of the Holy Spirit.
May he bless us and purify our hearts
and cure the sicknesses of our soul
and body. We adore you, O Christ,
with your good Father and the Holy
Spirit because you have come and
you have saved us.

SYRO-MARONITE FAREWELL TO THE ALTAR

Remain in peace, O Altar of God.
May the offering that I have taken
from you be for the remission of my
debts and the pardon of my sins and
may it obtain for me that I may stand
before the tribunal of Christ without
condemnation and without confu-
sion. I do not know if I will have
the opportunity to return and offer
another sacrifice upon you. Protect
me, O Lord, and preserve your holy
Church as the way to truth and
salvation. Amen.

BYZANTINE PRAYER FOR THE DECEASED

God of the spirits and of all flesh,
who have trampled death and anni-
hilated the devil and given life
to your world, may you yourself,
O Lord, grant to the soul of your
deceased servant N. rest in a place
of light, a verdant place, a place of
freshness, from where suffering, pain
and cries are far removed. Do You,
O good and compassionate God forgive every fault committed by him in
word, work or thought because there
is no man who lives and does not sin.
You alone are without sin and your
justice is justice throughout the ages
and your word is truth. Since you,
O Christ our God, are the resurrection, the life and the repose of your
deceased servant N., we give you
glory together with your un-begotten
Father and your most holy, good and
life-creating Spirit, now and always
and forever and ever.

ACT OF FAITH

O my God, I firmly believe that you are one God in three divine Persons, Father, Son, and Holy Spirit. I believe that your divine Son became man and died for our sins and that he will come to judge the living and the dead. I believe these and all the truths which the Holy Catholic Church teaches because you have revealed them who are eternal truth and wisdom, who can neither deceive nor be deceived. In this faith I intend to live and die. Amen.

ACT OF HOPE

O Lord God, I hope by your grace for the pardon of all my sins and after life here to gain eternal happiness because you have promised it who are infinitely powerful, faithful, kind, and merciful. In this hope I intend to live and die. Amen.

ACT OF LOVE

O Lord God, I love you above all things and I love my neighbor for your sake because you are the highest, infinite and perfect good, worthy of all my love. In this love I intend to live and die. Amen.

ACT OF CONTRITION

O my God, I am heartily sorry for having offended Thee, and I detest all my sins because of thy just punishments, but most of all because they offend Thee, my God, who art all good and deserving of all my love. I firmly resolve with the help of Thy grace to sin no more and to avoid the near occasion of sin. Amen.

ACTUS FIDEI

Dómine Deus, firma fide credo et confíteor ómnia et síngula quæ sancta Ecclésia Cathólica propónit, quia tu, Deus, ea ómnia revelásti, qui es ætérna véritas et sapiéntia quæ nec fállere nec falli potest. In hac fide vívere et mori státuo. Amen.

ACTUS SPEI

Dómine Deus, spero per grátiam tuam remissiónem ómnium peccatórum, et post hanc vitam ætérnam felicitátem me esse consecutúrum: quia tu promisísti, qui es infiníte potens, fidélis, benígnus, et miséricors. In hac spe vívere et mori státuo. Amen.

ACTUS CARITATIS

Dómine Deus, amo te super ómnia et próximum meum propter te, quia tu es summum, infinítum, et perfectíssimum bonum, omni dilectióne dignum. In hac caritáte vívere et mori státuo. Amen.

ACTUS CONTRITIONIS

Deus meus, ex toto corde pæ´nitet me ómnium meórum peccatórum, éaque detéstor, quia peccándo, non solum pœnas a te iuste statútas proméritus sum, sed præsértim quia offéndi te, summum bonum, ac dignum qui super ómnia diligáris. Ídeo fírmiter propóno, adiuvánte grátia tua, de cétero me non peccatúrum peccandíque occasiónes próximas fugitúrum. Amen.

B. FORMULAS OF CATHOLIC DOCTRINE

THE TWO COMMANDMENTS OF LOVE

1. You shall love the Lord your God with all your heart, with all your soul, and with all your mind.
2. You shall love your neighbor as yourself.

THE GOLDEN RULE (cf. Mt 7:12)

Do to others as you would have them do to you.

THE BEATITUDES (cf. Mt 5:3-12)

Blessed are the poor in spirit, for theirs is the kingdom of heaven.

Blessed are they who mourn, for they will be comforted.

Blessed are the meek, for they will inherit the earth.

Blessed are they who hunger and thirst for righteousness, for they will be satisfied.

Blessed are the merciful, for they will be shown mercy.

Blessed are the pure of heart, for they will see God.

Blessed are the peacemakers, for they will be called children of God.

Blessed are those who are persecuted for righteousness' sake, for theirs is the kingdom of heaven.

Blessed are you when people revile you and persecute you and utter all kinds of evil against you falsely on my account. Rejoice and be glad, for your reward will be great in heaven.

THE THREE THEOLOGICAL VIRTUES

1. Faith
2. Hope
3. Charity

THE FOUR CARDINAL VIRTUES

1. Prudence
2. Justice
3. Fortitude
4. Temperance

THE SEVEN GIFTS OF THE HOLY SPIRIT

1. Wisdom
2. Understanding
3. Counsel
4. Fortitude
5. Knowledge
6. Piety
7. Fear of the Lord

THE TWELVE FRUITS OF THE HOLY SPIRIT

1. Charity
2. Joy
3. Peace
4. Patience
5. Kindness
6. Goodness
7. Generosity
8. Gentleness
9. Faithfulness
10. Modesty
11. Self-control
12. Chastity

THE FIVE PRECEPTS OF THE CHURCH

1. You shall attend Mass on Sundays and on holy days of obligation and remain free from work or activity that could impede the sanctification of such days.
2. You shall confess your sins at least once a year.
3. You shall receive the sacrament of the Eucharist at least during the Easter season.
4. You shall observe the days of fasting and abstinence established by the Church.
5. You shall help to provide for the needs of the Church.

THE SEVEN CORPORAL WORKS OF MERCY

1. Feed the hungry.
2. Give drink to the thirsty.
3. Clothe the naked.
4. Shelter the homeless.
5. Visit the sick.
6. Visit the imprisoned.
7. Bury the dead.

THE SEVEN SPIRITUAL WORKS OF MERCY

1. Counsel the doubtful.
2. Instruct the ignorant.
3. Admonish sinners.
4. Comfort the afflicted.
5. Forgive offenses.
6. Bear wrongs patiently.
7. Pray for the living and the dead.

THE SEVEN CAPITAL SINS

1. Pride
2. Covetousness
3. Lust
4. Anger
5. Gluttony
6. Envy
7. Sloth

THE FOUR LAST THINGS

1. Death
2. Judgment
3. Hell
4. Heaven

INDEX

Numbers correspond to questions in Compendium